Publishing Beyond the Market

DIGITAL CULTURE BOOKS

The Digital Culture Books series is committed to liberatory and transformational scholarship that critiques and works toward repairing historical and ongoing harm and imagines more just and equitable futures. With this series, the University of Michigan Press is seeking books that apply the insights and tools of intersectional feminist studies, queer studies, critical race studies, critical ethnic studies, critical disability studies, and related fields to the study of digital culture. As part of the series' focus on the digital and the Press's commitment to accessibility, books will be published simultaneously in print and open access e-book versions with multimedia capabilities.

TITLES IN THE SERIES

Publishing Beyond the Market: Open Access, Care, and the Commons
Samuel A. Moore

Sensing Health: Bodies, Data, and Digital Health Technologies
Mikki Kressbach

Collecting Lives: Critical Data Narrative as Modernist Aesthetic in Early Twentieth-Century U.S. Literatures
Elizabeth Rodrigues

Publishing Beyond the Market

OPEN ACCESS, CARE, AND THE COMMONS

Samuel A. Moore

University of Michigan Press
ANN ARBOR

Published in the United States of America by the
University of Michigan Press
First published September 2025

A CIP catalog record for this book is available from the British Library.

Library of Congress Cataloging-in-Publication Data

Names: Moore, Samuel A., author. | Michigan Publishing (University of Michigan), publisher.
Title: Publishing beyond the market : open access, care, and the commons / Samuel A. Moore.
Description: Ann Arbor : University of Michigan Press, 2025. | Series: Digital culture books | Includes bibliographical references (pages 18–13) and index.
Identifiers: LCCN 2025003785 (print) | LCCN 2025003786 (ebook) | ISBN 9780472057634 (paperback) | ISBN 9780472905225 (ebook other)
Subjects: LCSH: Open access publishing. | Scholarly publishing. | Publishers and publishing. | Periodicals—Publishing.
Classification: LCC Z286.063 M66 2025 (print) | LCC Z286.063 (ebook) | DDC 070.5—dc23/eng/20250512
LC record available at https://lccn.loc.gov/2025003785
LC ebook record available at https://lccn.loc.gov/2025003786

DOI: https://doi.org/10.3998/mpub.11781635

The University of Michigan Press's open access publishing program is made possible thanks to additional funding from the University of Michigan Office of the Provost and the generous support of contributing libraries.

Cover image: Reinhold Leitner / Shutterstock.com

Authorized Representative: Easy Access System Europe, Mustamäe tee 50, 10621 Tallinn, Estonia, gpsr.requests@easproject.com

For Sierra and Marlow

Contents

Digital materials related to this title can be found on the Fulcrum platform via the following citable URL: https://doi.org/10.3998/mpub.11781635

Acknowledgments

This book emerges in part out of the joys and frustrations of my participation in various movements for open access publishing and free culture over the past fifteen years. I have learned from so many people in the open ecosystem, and I could not possibly name them all here. However, special thanks go to Joe Deville, Tim Elfenbein, Martin Eve, Rebekka Kiesewetter, Lucy Montgomery, Cameron Neylon, and Toby Steiner for their friendship and support for my work. I owe Gary Hall a huge debt of gratitude for mentoring me through my PhD and for the advice he has given since. I am also indebted to all the presses in the Radical Open Access Collective and hope I have done justice here to your excellent work.

Thanks also to my present and former colleagues at Cambridge, most notably Sacha Jones, Niamh Tumelty, Mandy Wigdorowitz, Anna Alexandrova, Siddharth Soni, Rupert Gatti, and everyone at the Office of Scholarly Communication. Thanks also go to the anonymous peer reviewers whose kind and generous feedback helped improve the book immeasurably, and to the staff of the University of Michigan Press for your expertise, patience, and professionalism, especially to Charles Watkinson, Sara Cohen, Haley Winkle, and Delilah McCrea.

Extra-special thanks go to my friend, coauthor, and co-conspirator Janneke Adema, whose thinking has helped shape this book in so many ways. Our collaborations have been the most enjoyable and productive part of my work as an academic and I look forward to thinking together with you in future.

Finally thank you to my parents, family, and friends for your love and support. Thanks most of all to Sierra Williams and Marlow Moore—to whom this book is dedicated—for showing me what it truly means to care.

Preface

In 2009 I began working as an editorial assistant for the fledgling not-for-profit publisher the Public Library of Science (PLOS). PLOS had pioneered a new publishing model for making research freely available to anyone with a stable internet connection, so-called open access publishing (OA). This new form of publishing purported to fix all the ills in publishing by "democratising" access to research, speeding up the pace of scientific innovation, and easing the pressures of declining library budgets. OA represented an exciting, ethical alternative to traditional subscription-based publishing, offering a range of possibilities for academic research dissemination and the future of the university, not just in the sciences but in the humanities, too.

But as OA increased in popularity, I saw how it became co-opted by commercial publishers who looked to profit from the success of this new approach to publishing. Open access is now a dominant force in academic publishing: it is big business to publishers who have sought to supplement their journal-subscription income through expensive article-processing charges and other extractive models. The commercialisation of open access has drastic implications for less well-funded disciplines, for junior researchers, and for those based outside of wealthy jurisdictions. Although research may soon be accessible to all, this might be at the expense of those who are actually able to publish it.

Simultaneously, as I began to think about OA from an academic perspective, I became interested in the work of DIY and grassroots humanities publishers at the margins. There is a rich tradition of open access publishing in the humanities and social sciences that stretches back to the birth of the Web. Based both inside and outside the university system, publishing books, journals, and experimental projects, these publishers foreground a different set of values and practices than those of the profit-seeking commercial publishing houses. While both approaches are predicated upon giving publications away for free, the open access landscape looks quite different from the perspective of a grassroots academic-led publisher like Open Humanities Press or a multinational corporation like Elsevier. The open access ecosystem is composed of a diversity of approaches to publishing, from for-profit publishers and smaller learned societies, to university presses, library-led publishers, and academic-led presses, and everything in between. The values of each approach are different, as are the practices themselves.

But as governments and funders around the world are increasingly mandating open access to research, it is necessary to take stock of this landscape and question whether open access is heading in the right direction, assessing its politics and trying to understand whether it can disrupt the values of the marketized university or if it simply reinforces them. This book represents my attempt to make sense of these questions through the lens of the scholarly commons.

Introduction

The Marketisation of Open Access

In December 2001, a coalition of sixteen individuals representing university libraries, research institutes, publishers, and charitable organisations came together in Budapest to launch a campaign to use digital technologies to facilitate public access to academic publications. In a short statement released the following year entitled the "Budapest Open Access Initiative" (BOAI), the group proclaimed:

> An old tradition and a new technology have converged to make possible an unprecedented public good. The old tradition is the willingness of scientists and scholars to publish the fruits of their research in scholarly journals without payment, for the sake of inquiry and knowledge. The new technology is the internet. The public good they make possible is the world-wide electronic distribution of the peer-reviewed journal literature and completely free and unrestricted access to it by all scientists, scholars, teachers, students, and other curious minds.[1]

With internet access becoming increasingly common across the world, and electronic distribution a growing practice for academic research articles, the BOAI signatories affirmed their commitment to the public's right to freely read and use academic publications, what they termed "open access" (OA). Arguing that the costs would be "far lower" than traditional pay-to-access forms of publishing, the signatories claimed that OA had the potential to "accelerate research, enrich education, share the learning of the rich with the poor and the poor with the rich, make this literature as useful as it can be, and lay the foundation for uniting humanity in a common intellectual conversation and quest for knowledge."[2]

These were grand claims, no doubt, but they were convincing to many people involved in academic publishing and research communication. Over twenty years later, OA is now well on its way to becoming the dominant method for publishing academic research. Across the world, governments, funders, and universities are mandating public access to research through books, journals, and repositories, and publishers have responded to these calls through a host of new models for OA. By 2025 it is estimated that almost half of *all research articles ever published* will be freely accessible, up from 31 percent in 2019.[3] Academic publishing is currently undergoing a revolution that will have profound implications for research access, dissemination, and assessment in all disciplines for years to come.

The practice of publishing itself has always been a multi-stakeholder endeavour, a negotiation between academics, university administrators, publishers, libraries, policymakers, and many other actors from civil society and beyond. Yet over the past few decades the inequities in the system meant that power has gravitated away from individual researchers towards the marketized publishing industry. Propped up by university hiring criteria and the steady decline of secure academic employment, the need for researchers to publish in prestigious journals and presses has never been stronger. This means that the private industry of commercial for-profit and nonprofit publishers holds great power over research dissemination and the trajectory of researcher careers, power that they use to generate revenue and consolidate their control over the scholarly record.

Though it is not by itself able to change the broader political-economic conditions for academic precarity and publish-or-perish cultures, many of the motivations for OA are responding, either implicitly or explicitly, to a culture of austerity brought on by the neoliberalisation of higher education in Europe, the USA, and elsewhere: journal prices rise above inflation while library budgets flatline; the amount that researchers have to publish to prove their scholarly worth is increasing; researchers outside the confines of well-stocked libraries in the Global North cannot access the research they need. Different approaches to OA may increase the inequalities of the publishing system, they may militate against them, or they may leave things unchanged. In any case, it is important to consider how new methods of OA publishing exist during a political moment in which higher education has been weakened by the turn towards market forms of measurement in all aspects of contemporary life. This state of affairs will have important shaping effects for the transformation currently underway in digital publishing.

This is to say that, as we shall see throughout this book, OA has a politics and can conform to a range of different ideologies.[4] Its politics is not specific or defined, but differs according to a variety of actors, situations, and projects, representing a site of struggle for the OA "movement" at large. The political (ideological) underpinnings of OA are compounded by the fact that it is also an object of policy by international and governmental funders around the world. Public access to research is something that governments around the world *want*, even if the motivations and methods of achieving it differ dramatically between jurisdictions. Some want to showcase their research, while others want to ensure access to all their citizens. For advocates of OA, who themselves are not united in their aims, the policy landscape necessitates a range of tactics, strategies, and alliances for advancing their cause. For example, one of the main distinctions in OA discourse is between green and gold forms of OA. *Green OA* is provided by repositories—usually in parallel with a traditional paid-access publication provided by a publisher—while *gold OA* is where the final version is provided by the publisher at the point of publication. Gold OA is often associated with article-processing charges whereby authors pay for publication, although the term specifically refers to any publication that a publisher makes freely and permanently available as the version of record.

The green/gold distinction has been the subject of much debate over the past few decades as different advocates and stakeholders proposed paths forward for OA. Early advocates such as Stevan Harnad proposed a system of green OA based on institutional repositories that would operate in parallel to the traditional system of publishing. This system would eventually apply pressure to publishers who would ultimately become little more than organisers of peer review.[5] In contrast, in the wake of the BOAI declaration, other practitioners focused more on providing OA through journals themselves, primarily through the pay-to-publish systems developed and popularised by biomedical publishers such as PLOS and BioMedCentral (later purchased by Springer Nature). This system has upended traditional publishing and has transformed the business models of publishers to prioritise publishing an increasing number of articles as quickly as possible, with obvious adverse effects on publishing as a whole.

Other debates have focused on whether research articles should be licenced not just for reading but for reuse too, reflective of one of the distinct lineages of OA that emerged from open-source software cultures.[6] Should people be able to take all or part of a research article, combine it with others, and package it for commercial gain? This might decrease friction in the publication process by reducing the need to seek individual permission to reuse copyrighted images, but it could also open academic research to greater extraction and exploitation by commercial organisations, not least in the context of generative AI technologies that require huge corpuses of training data that companies want to acquire for as little as possible. There are also different justifications for OA, as we shall see, pertaining to the value of extending research access to a broader public, to lowering the cost of publishing, to reining in publisher profits, and to increasing citations of academic work.

Similarly, debates and practices have focused on the extent to which researchers should be mandated to publish OA by their funders and institutions, often predicated on ideas of the collective good, or whether this imposition in some way inhibits individual academic freedom to publish entirely in their manner of choosing.[7] There are also considerations about the *immediacy* of access. To what extent are embargoes acceptable for green OA? Or should we insist that all research be released immediately on publication? Many of these issues exhibit a tendency towards pragmatism and consensus building, while others are about more radical incentivisation that can be achieved through the redistribution of funding with universities. This means that the turn towards OA has not been purely consensual and represents a multitude of views, alliances, and struggles.

It is important, then, to understand that OA does not have a fixed meaning or stable politics, but in many ways reflects a variety of positions on what the future of academic publishing should be in a digital age. My own position is that while public access to knowledge is a good thing, the debates on the specific definitions and routes to OA are less important than the opportunity OA offers more generally to reconfigure publishing towards more ethical processes and outcomes. More specifically, the fact that OA is in the process of upending all of academic publishing offers research communities the opportunity to intervene and enact a counter-hegemonic strategy towards commercial publishing more generally. This means that the flux of the practices that operate under the "open" banner, mixed with the fact that "open" itself is a floating signifier with no fixed meaning, creates the conditions for a range of experiments in the future of publishing.

Yet if OA has such a variety of meanings and ideological leanings, how has it managed to transform the academic publishing industry to such a great extent? Who is actually controlling this revolution, who *should* control it, and how can they do so? These are important questions to ask if we want to understand whether and how OA might conform to a radical bottom-up politics that is resistant to the marketisation of higher education and able to work towards something more transformative for scholarship and the dissemination of knowledge. Certain approaches to OA may merely rehearse the values of the neoliberal university, and many of them certainly do, while others may attempt to subvert them or do both at the same time. This book explores the various ideological bases of this transformation to OA and makes an argument for different approaches to it that can both promote and result in collective action for broader change in publishing and higher education.

Put another way, is it possible to conceive of the different projects that make up the OA landscape as a *commons*? Simply defined, commons are shared, complex resources that, as Ostrom and Hess describe, are "subject to social dilemmas."[8] The study of commons concerns the various ways that communities self-organise to produce resources that may be shared exclusively between groups of people or, particularly in the case of digital resources, made freely available to all. Commons concern practices of self-governance by defined communities; they refer to how communities of people can collaborate to produce and manage the resources they use, the rules and norms they adhere to, the conflicts that ensue, and the ways of resolving these disputes. Academic publishing, as I argue throughout the book, is the product of the self-organised labour of editorial collectives and would benefit from greater self-governance and horizontal organisation. Yet this self-organisation is currently mediated and extracted by commercial organisations in a way that neutralises its commons potential.

Much like with open access publishing, arguments in favour of the commons run the political gamut of approaches and justifications. The commons can be about self-sustainability and freedom from the state, leading neoliberal entities such as the World Bank to argue for the promotion of community control of land in economically developing nations as a stepping stone from state ownership to privatisation.[9] While from a more liberal perspective, the Nobel Prize–winning economist Elinor Ostrom devoted her career to the study of common-resource management by collectives of (what she theorised as) rational, self-interested actors.[10] Finally, from a left perspective, the commons has been invoked by a wide range of theorists looking to explore the potential of self-governance as a way to transition away from capitalism and reclaim a "commonwealth."[11] These are just a handful of examples of the politics of research on the commons, which I will return to in a variety of ways throughout the book. Suffice it to say, the literature on the commons does not simply outline a movement from one specific economic mode of production to another.

Ideas of the commons are present in much of the discussion around OA. Organisations such as Creative Commons, which produces licences for sharing digital resources, and products like Elsevier's Digital Commons repository software imply an association between the commons and the publications made available as open access resources. There are numerous explicit references to open access as a form of knowledge commons,[12] scholarly commons,[13] or intellectual commons,[14] and the term is used in a range of ways to describe everything from freely accessible publications to global systems for managing all the world's knowledge.[15] The commons is often invoked because it has positive associations with ideas of commonality, resource-sharing, and shared enterprise, even if the resources being described were created purely within the capitalist mode of production and bear little resemblance to the commons as often understood. It is therefore what Ernesto Laclau would term a "floating signifier"—a term whose meaning is "suspended" until it is articulated in a political context.[16] Floating signifiers are used in the construction of political identity to organise around a particular concept. They are loosely defined, but take on a meaning in a particular context, much like the term "open" itself.[17]

It is my contention in this book that despite the frequent association of OA with "the commons," much more work is needed to understand the importance of self-governance, sharing and mutual reliance for academic publishing. I am here trying to concretise ideas of the commons and give them more specificity within academic publishing. This will entail more than just appreciating publications as freely accessible resources, but also understanding their modes of production and relationships with the state and capital, the actors involved in creating and using these resources ("commoners"), and the unique subjectivities and practices that arise from these shared ways of being ("commoning"). Without an appreciation of all three of these elements—common resources, the commoners, and practices of commoning—any analysis of the relationship between the commons and OA will be incomplete at best, as the next chapter illustrates.

The chapters in this book each work towards an assessment of the OA landscape and its potential to promote common ways of working, producing, and being with one another; to experiment with the ways in which research is produced and disseminated; and to work towards a better university more generally. They do this through analysis of the multitude of practices and discourses that comprise the OA landscape as it exists today. These practices exist in policymaking, commercial academic publishing, scholar-led presses, university presses, and a host of other spheres. The discourse exists as policy directives, opinion pieces, blog posts, interviews, and the growing scholarly literature on OA. Examining this landscape, with specific but not exclusive focus on the humanities and social sciences, will help us understand who is currently shaping and controlling OA, in accordance with what conditions and values, which will allow us to determine whether and how OA can be framed along the lines of a scholarly commons.

Unlike the rich body of work that makes a case for a certain form of OA and its wider benefits,[18] I am interested more in seeing whether OA might be oriented to nurture a radical commons-based approach to knowledge production and dissemination. I am therefore taking it is axiomatic that publications within any commons-based system of publishing should be freely accessible as standard and that it is the commercial element that must be eradicated or left behind. This is to say that if it is possible to fund the creation and dissemination of academic publications without recourse to informational capitalism, then there is no reason for the artificial scarcity that market-based systems rely on. We can work towards "commoning" publishing in a way that will also make academic publications free for all. I am therefore not arguing for OA as *the* end point of any new systems of publishing, nor am I making a case for a particular definition of OA publishing. This book is all about how to return control to academic communities, away from the privatised publishing industry.

Yet for many researchers, including the historian Peter Baldwin, the idea of open access is a separate issue from resistance to commercial cultures of knowledge production. Instead, he writes, "attacking open access by lambasting modern industrial capitalism is akin to complaining about gravity when feeling weary."[19] While I am not attacking OA in this book, I do think it is important to explore how to nurture cultures of publishing that do not simply conform to or arise from the standards of capitalism. I am therefore making an appeal to those of us who broadly share a progressive or left politics that open access to research is not enough to fulfil these radical aims: we must attend, not just to free access to digital resources, but *to how these resources are produced, too*. This is where the commons is helpful as a touchstone.

The Marketisation of Publishing (and Everything Else)

To understand the possibilities of commons-based researcher control within academic publishing, it is necessary to first explore how open access is both *responding to* and *implicated within* the marketisation of publishing. Publishing is at the heart of everything an academic does and shapes much of the structure and rhythm of scholarly life. Projects are undertaken with specific publication formats in mind, journals are often chosen based on how well they are regarded by assessment panels, and there is a hierarchy of certain kinds of academic publication defined by both unwritten notions of prestige and dubiously calculated quantitative metrics such as the Impact Factor.[20] Academics typically do not expect remuneration for their involvement in the publishing process, either as editors, authors, or peer reviewers, meaning that the labour and content that underpin academic publishing are largely provided to academic publishers for free. Instead, the work of publishing and the content that academics provide are considered part of the work of an employed academic, even though secure academic employment is increasingly difficult to obtain, and many researchers provide this work on top of their precarious contracts. Rather than monetary reward, academics publish, review, and edit research as both service to their discipline and in return for various forms of credit and prestige that can be displayed on their CVs.

Borrowing terminology from Pierre Bourdieu, Martin Eve explores the relationship between prestige and publishing with respect to the "symbolic capital" that a certain publisher's reputation confers:

> A piece of research work is a demonstration of an author's cultural capital; it is the product of the skill, knowledge and ability of the author(s). The acceptance of such research by publishers who possess both material capital (needed to undertake the labour and effectively disseminate the work) and cultural capital (knowledge of publishing and academic systems) constitutes a payoff in the form of social capital (endorsement and support) for the author that can be reconverted back into symbolic capital (prestige/reputation) that is needed for peer respect and a job/promotion (material capital).[21]

This overview of the various kinds of symbolic capital at work in academic publishing explains the impact of prestige on academic decisions about where to publish. Academics strive for their work to appear in prestigious venues because doing so represents a form of symbolic capital within higher education that can be used for career progress. Because of this, publishing is not just about the quality of the journal, its editorial standards, or its political leaning and audience, but also about the perceived quality of the journal in the eyes of those in charge of academic careers, who may not be those with an intimate knowledge of the work itself. As a consequence, publications and presses have become proxies for the value of the research in question, meaning that having an article published in a well-regarded journal or a monograph published with a prestigious press is representative of the research's quality and, by extension, the researcher themself. The fact that journals are simultaneously both proxies for researcher quality and conduits for research communication means that academics are keen to publish in the "best" journals, while libraries must continue to subscribe to as many of them as possible to have as broad a coverage of the literature as possible. This has had disastrous commercial outcomes for universities and libraries specifically.

Academic publishing is predominantly governed by private, commercial organisations and shaped by market forces, while publications are commodities traded for both financial and symbolic capital. The academic publishing industry is composed of a small number of large commercial publishers—notably Elsevier, Wiley, Springer Nature, and Taylor & Francis—and a large number of smaller publishers, comprising university presses, not-for-profit publishers, learned societies, smaller commercial publishers, and many more entities. The oligopoly within publishing, as it is frequently described, is well represented by the fact that in 2013 five publishers accounted for more than 50 percent of all academic papers published.[22] A small number of publishers therefore exercise significant market power and control much of the publishing landscape. Under OA forms of publishing, this is changing, and new commercial entrants such as MDPI and Frontiers now take an additional market share of publications.[23]

Consolidation and acquisitions are also features of academic publishing, something that is common in mature markets. Bigger publishers look to drive growth by purchasing smaller players who can increase the number of publications they own, but also by buying companies that will expand their operations into the entire research life cycle.[24] This opens up markets within research data, user data, and other parts of the end-to-end research process. Elsevier, for example, now refers to itself as a "data analytics company" rather than a publisher, showing the direction of travel for bigger commercial publishers to hoover up and monetise as much data as possible. For Jefferson Pooley, this means that publishing is its own "emerging surveillance economy," as the focus of publishers is less on producing content and more on extracting data through any means necessary.[25]

The concentration within the academic publishing industry persists because academic libraries are required to subscribe to the contents of scholarly journals while also supporting the transition to open access. As Neylon et al. note, the publishing industry exhibits monopoly-like behaviour because individual publications are not "substitutable"—i.e., they are all unique—and so libraries must subscribe to as many of them as possible to provide a comprehensive body of literature.[26] Ownership of this growing corpus of scholarly literature means that publishers charge increasing sums for publications that libraries need to access. In the late 1990s, publishers invented what is now known as the "Big Deal" to bundle journal subscriptions into packages to which libraries would subscribe.[27] These packages locked libraries into multiyear subscription packages, the price of which rapidly outpaced inflation, and helped large commercial publishers receive profit margins of more than 30 percent.[28] From 1986 to 2011, North American libraries went from spending roughly 25 percent of their budget on journal subscriptions to almost 75 percent, a situation that came to be known as the "serials crisis."[29]

Offering the prospect of free research for all, OA was initially positioned as something that would help counter the serials crisis. From the BOAI discussion above, we see that lowering the costs of publishing was embedded in early arguments for OA. Early advocates saw the transition from print to digital as one that would make academic publications cheaper to produce and free to distribute, thus giving the publishing market an incentive to compete to lower the costs of publishing.[30] One such approach was the article-processing-charge business (APC) model that was to explode in popularity in the late 2000s and remains the dominant method of OA provision today.[31] Often called "author pays," APCs are charged by publishers to authors at the time their article is published online. The APC model assumes that authors can pay the cost of publishing—often totalling thousands of pounds—out of their research grants. For this reason, APCs have been popularised in the grant-funded scientific disciplines, namely biomedical disciplines, and have been less successfully adopted in the humanities and social sciences. This is changing, however, with the rise of publishing agreements between universities and publishers that bundle the cost of reading and publishing articles into one payment by the university.

If APCs were intended to create a competitive market of author-pays publishing, encouraging new entrants and a diversity of players in the process, they have roundly failed. Today, three publishers receive almost half of the total article-processing charges reported by almost 250 universities in the OpenAPC database.[32] While this database does not illustrate the size of the market, it does reveal its relative homogeneity and dominance by a handful of large publishers. That said, the publishing consultancy Delta Think estimated that the market grew to just over $2 billion in 2022, while Haustein and colleagues estimated that $8.349 billion was spent on APCs with the top six publishers in the period 2019–2023.[33] Having reinforced the dominance of publishing by a minority of publishers, APCs are clearly big business for commercial publishers, many of whom continue to rely on subscription income while reorienting their business models to receive as many APC-based articles as possible with as little human input as possible. This means that publishers are in the business of maximising volume and technological scale in order to profit from APCs as much as they can.

The dominance of a small number of players is a result of a culture in higher education that requires academics to publish in prestigious outlets to further their careers. Publishing is not just about communicating research, it is also a form of symbolic capital that researchers may exchange to further their careers. Publications connote prestige through their imprimaturs, Impact Factors, and brand names, which for the most part are concentrated in commercial publishing houses. This means that publishers can raise subscription prices because libraries are strongly incentivised to keep providing access to important journals, especially while authors are required to publish in them. It also means that researchers who do have access to APC funding—those in wealthy countries and universities—are not price-sensitive when it comes to paying APCs, because they are spending other people's money (from their funder or university) and receive greater returns through appearing in prestigious venues. Consequently, there is a strong correlation between journal prestige and price of APC.[34] This situation also exacerbates existing epistemic inequalities around who is able to participate in academic knowledge production, particularly those outside of well-resourced universities and localities.[35]

The problems of marketisation in open access and subscription publishing are exacerbated by a similar strategy of marketisation and neoliberalisation of higher education across the globe. As neoliberal governments withdraw funding from higher education, universities are forced to perform as businesses, conforming to market logic through competition and the need for academics to be financially sustainable through their own grant income. A new layer of managers and administrators has instilled the values and processes of the private sector in much of higher education, particularly in the UK and USA, and there is an increasing focus on "performance" and "outcomes" as indicators of quality.[36] Publication is one important disciplinary mechanism through which performance is measured, forcing academics to publish widely and regularly for their own job security. This individualism can be understood in Foucauldian terms as academics needing to be *entrepreneurs of themselves* under neoliberalism: "being for himself his own capital, being for himself his own producer, being for himself the source of

[his] earnings."[37] The university is a site of precarity in which academics are forced to continuously prove their worth through a series of audits and performance measures—and publications are a key part of this. It is notable, as mentioned above, that publishers themselves are also rapidly broadening their business models to becoming owners of data analytics to calculate and predict researcher performance in order to sell these "insights" back to universities for performance management.[38]

Competition for fewer academic jobs thus maintains conservatism in publishing practice and allows a handful of publishers to maintain commercial control over publishing and associated digital infrastructures. This is what it means to say that publishing has been *marketised*: publishing is primarily controlled by private, revenue-generating organisations (for-profit and nonprofit) who must operate in accordance with a logic that prioritises individual economic freedom over all else. Academic publishing is thus reflective of the turn to neoliberalism that is the dominant mode of governance for Western politics. Under neoliberalism, political logic is economic logic and political decision-making intends to promote market-based outcomes. As Wendy Brown writes: "all conduct is economic conduct; all spheres of existence are framed and measured by economic terms and metrics, even when those spheres are not directly monetized."[39] This is the rationality of neoliberal governance.

Publishing was not always controlled by commercial organisations. Aileen Fyfe et al. show how postwar publishing was dominated by university presses and learned societies, for whom economic returns were not prioritised.[40] University presses were subsidised by their host institution, while learned-society presses gave copies of their journals away to libraries and universities.

It was not until the 1980s that commercialisation of academic publishing took hold, most notably through the business savvy of Robert Maxwell, whose Pergamon Press (later purchased by Elsevier) launched numerous titles to which libraries would subscribe provided that the journals were credible, international, and broad in focus.[41] Since this period, the publishing industry has become more profiteering and concentrated, much as mature industries tend to consolidate more generally. Academic publishing is indicative of capitalism working as expected, not in a broken manner.

Despite such consolidation, there is still a strong tradition in scholarly publishing of university and learned-society presses, the aims of which are scholarly rather than merely profit-seeking. Learned societies are also, in principle, answerable to their members, and many societies use revenue from publishing to fund travel grants, conferences, and other scholarly activities. University presses are answerable—and often subsidised—by their host institutions, meaning they have a commitment to particular areas of scholarship such as local interest and niche areas of the humanities. University presses in the USA are particularly valued for their monograph-publishing programmes, many of which would not be sustainable without subsidy.

But the withdrawal and reduction of press subsidies is exactly what has happened at many universities, forcing presses to rely increasingly on market returns from their publishing programmes.[42] This means that presses now consider the economic potential of a manuscript, rather than simply its scholarly potential, leading them to prioritise certain fashionable and financially viable proposals at the expense of others. The university press was originally conceived as an important part of the university's mission, publishing works with little expectation of a return on investment. Writing in 1967, Gene R. Hawes argued how such subsidies allowed university presses to publish books that would otherwise "not appear," but that they could do so "only when the press has some form of subsidy from its university—its quarters, often its internal services, and sometimes part or all of its payroll subsidized by the university."[43] Humanities publishing, particularly monograph publishing, can be a highly specialized, editorially intensive undertaking, requiring a significant capital investment from the press. A report by the Ithaka consultancy puts the average cost to produce a university press monograph at $39,892, comprising staff time, overheads, production costs, marketing, editorial support, and the like.[44] As subsidies receive increased scrutiny from their host institutions, and monograph sales decrease, university presses are forced to adapt to the new commercial environment by publishing titles with the intent of commercial success.

In the turn towards marketisation, learned-society publishing efforts have been affected differently than university presses. Unlike university presses, many learned societies outsource much of their publishing operation to large commercial publishers. This means that societies benefitted from the serials crisis, because they were given progressively higher returns from the commercial publishers that they use to fund their activities. Some societies maintain healthy bank balances because of these partnerships. For example, in 2017 the Federation of European Biochemical Societies, a large society publisher with an agreement with Wiley to publish their journals, had an overall balance of €62,241,920 and an annual income of €6,269,136 (up from €5,234,426 in 2016), of which a significant portion was derived from the Wiley partnership.[45] These figures are not necessarily representative of learned-society financial situations more generally, although Johnson and Fosci illustrate that 279 learned societies they studied made a total of £1.2 billion in 2013, of which 26 percent was derived from publishing activities.[46] In the UK, Rob Johnson and Elle Malcolmson found that learned societies who partnered with commercial organisations tend to receive less revenue from publishing than societies who opted to self-publish their journals.[47] This points to an environment in which commercial organisations return less money to societies in order to mitigate the consequences of unfavourable market conditions.

So, although there are winners and losers in marketisation, it is important to understand that few areas of academic publishing and higher education are spared by it, as is true of society more generally. Academics are locked into a system that is beholden to private, revenue-seeking entities and a culture of proving one's worth through financial self-sustainability. This means that research communities do not control the presses with which they publish, the infrastructures that shape these publications, or the ways in which their research is assessed.

I have already discussed how open access—particularly APC-based approaches to it—may conform to the values of neoliberalism, which is to say the form of governance that promotes market-based outcomes and processes as its main rationality. Proponents of APCs seek to encourage a competitive market of publishing services whereby price-sensitive authors make decisions to publish based on rational, self-interested choices. This, for example, was the logic of the UK's OA policy framework, much of which was based on the report "Accessibility, Sustainability, Excellence: How to Expand Access to Research Publications" (the "Finch Report"). Commissioned by the then Conservative minister for Higher Education, David Willetts, the authors of the report argued:

> [O]ne of the advantages of open access publishing is that it brings greater transparency about the costs, and the price, of publication and dissemination. The measures we recommend will bring greater competition on price as well as the status of the journals in which researchers wish to publish. We therefore expect market competition to intensify, and that universities and funders should be able to use their power as purchasers to bear down on the costs to them both of APCs and of subscriptions.[48]

Imbued in this passage is the neoliberal language of "transparency," "competition," and purchasing "power." The authors of the Finch Report were keen to emphasise the benefits of article-processing charges to promote lower prices through free-market participation. The resulting policy from Research Councils United Kingdom did indeed mandate immediate, journal-based open access ("gold" OA) that is achieved primarily by APCs funded by public money.[49] For Philip Mirowski, this is an illustration of neoliberalism par excellence. He writes, "it is crucial here to recall the first commandment of neoliberal economics: if a market activity (here, commercialized science) seems to be failing, the preferred solution is always to introduce more markets."[50] While there is widespread agreement that the market for academic publishing is not competitive and needs to be addressed, market creation is the primary tool in the policy-maker's toolbox.

Irrespective of whether APCs do drive down prices—and there is evidence to suggest that they do not (see above)—it is clear that OA has been marketized to a considerable extent. This means that control of publishing is in the hands of private organisations, and the primary way by which researchers currently influence this industry is by the exercise of market power through decisions to publish. Academics receive no direct remuneration for publishing in academic journals, alongside limited royalties for book publishing, all while performing uncompensated editorial labour for publishers themselves. Coupled with the popularity of processing charges, commercial academic publishers have furthered their dominance within the brave new world of open access, leaving scholarly communication hostage to commercial forces in the process.

Publishing Beyond the Market

But does it have to be this way? Is there a possibility that open access could help return control of scholarly communication to academics, libraries, and research communities, away from control by commercial organisations and market forces? Alongside the commercial dominance of OA, many interventions into the publishing market have the specific intention of making publishing accountable to the university and stimulating practices of cooperation and mutual reliance over competition and profit-maximisation. Exploring policy mandates, collaborative infrastructure design, researcher-led publishing, and new systems of governance, this book makes an argument for how these interventions can reorient open access publishing along the lines of a *commons*.

When talking about the potential for publishing to be a

commons, I mean loosely how it might be controlled by and answerable to different research communities, how publishing processes may be guided by ethical rather than commercial outcomes, and how the outputs may be shared with all. As we shall see in the first chapter, "the commons" is a varied term that refers to a wide range of practices. Yet one theme that remains consistent is the commons as a site of collaborative governance by a defined group of people ("commoners"). Commons theorists De Angelis and Stavrides argue that the commons prioritises self-reliance and self-organisation over market and state modes of production.[51] This does not mean that the commons is "outside" the market or the state—because no such place exists—but rather that the interplay between all three modes of production in the commons foregrounds self-organisation over private and public forms of production.

The commons does not necessarily entail free sharing of the resource produced, although this is often how the concept is used. For example, in his chapter "Creating an Intellectual Commons through Open Access," the open access advocate Peter Suber argues that "OA literature is a commons because free use is pre-authorized."[52] Suber's understanding of the commons relates to the outputs, publications in this case, that are accessible and reusable by anyone with a stable internet connection. But this understanding of the commons is insufficient, because it does not account for the mode of production that creates these resources. Although the resources generated through common modes of production may indeed be freely accessible to all (as is the case of open-access commons), this is by no means a perquisite for a commons. Instead, a commons is better thought of as a "a complex ecosystem," following Ostrom and Hess's definition, "a resource shared by a group of people that is subject to social dilemmas."[53]

When conceived in this way, it becomes clear that the commons refers not just to the resource but also to the "social dilemmas" that go into creating, maintaining, and sharing this resource; the rules for governance; and the ways that people collaborate and relate to one another. As a mode of production, then, the commons is about how groups of people can work together to create something for their own use (and the use of others) without much thought to profit-making through a market, although sustainability is of course a key concern. The commons is also about self-organisation and cooperation, and so it has less concern with the state as funder and sustainer of governmental approaches to resource maintenance. Again, however, it is vital to note that the state is still a key actor in how it influences commons-based resources, as we shall in the discussion of the European funder policy "Plan S" in chapter 2.

Beyond the idea of the commons as focused merely on resources, I deploy a more expansive concept that is attentive to common resources, the people who maintain the resource (the "commoners"), and most crucially, the forms of collective subjectivity and relating to one another that such maintenance entails (so-called practices of commoning). In foregrounding practices of commoning, I hope to show that the commons mode of production is a process of reimagining how we relate to one another within the university through the open access publications we create. This requires attention to both the resource generated *and* the ways in which commoners collaborate. As Gibson-Graham et al. write, commoning involves "establishing rules or protocols for access and use, taking care of and accepting responsibility for a resource, and distributing the benefits in ways that take into account the well-being of others."[54]

For Gibson-Graham et al., commoning represents the possibilities of a "postcapitalist politics." It points to new ways of relating with one another in order to work through the problems inherent in neoliberal capitalism. For the purposes at hand, this is what I mean by *publishing beyond the market* and the potential of open access to reorient publishing towards something shaped and governed by different research communities in a variety of ways that are unbeholden to capitalism. The ideas of the commons and commoning developed here are intended to theorise the possibilities of publishing that is emancipatory from commercial forms of production and will work towards cooperation and mutual reliance within higher education. A couple of important methodological points follow.

Ethics of Care

One way to think through the impact of marketisation on publishing is to interrogate its tendency to smooth over and homogenise difference and local, diverse contexts. The capitalist supply chain encourages economies of scale that indiscriminately funnel all things through its processes and standards. In publishing, this has a tendency to result in sameness and cookie-cutter approaches that preclude experimental practices that diverge from the norm. But publishing and research is a situated practice, the relational side to which must be attended to and cared for: the labour, the content, the materiality, the locality, and the interrelations between all these elements. In opposition to detached and universalising understandings of ethics that ignore this situatedness, this book is guided by an ethical commitment to *care*.

One way of conceptualising care is, following Annemarie Mol, as an ordering logic that operates on a continuum between *choice* and *care*. For Mol, writing specifically about healthcare provision, logics of choice "draw a limit," whereas care is an "open-ended" process—the two are in constant tension within medical care.[55] Choice is individuating while care is collectivising, the former finding itself well suited to market-based (neoliberal) forms of decision-making that prioritise individual choice as the guarantor of freedom. I am interested in care in this book because of the importance it places on process over outputs, cultures over outcomes. What, for example, does it mean to care for our publishing practices and the diversity of contexts, identities, and relationships that go into research dissemination? What would it look like for open access to facilitate a more caring approach to publishing?

From an ethical-political perspective, care was originally theorised by feminist theorists Tronto and Fisher in the following way:

> On the most general level, we suggest that caring can be viewed as a *species activity that includes everything we do to maintain, continue, and repair our "world" so that we can live in it as well as possible*. That world includes our bodies, our selves, and our environment, all of which we seek to interweave in a complex, life-sustaining web.[56]

Care thus concerns maintenance, repair, and other forms of labour often positioned as "feminised." It is a feminist ethics that emphasises maintenance as both ethically important and politically valuable, highlighting the inequalities inherent in neoliberalism's tendency to devalue maintenance and care work, particularly as performed by women and minorities. The maintenance aspect of care is why I theorise it alongside a commitment to the commons mode of production. Caring is well theorised as a practice of "commoning" because of this focus on maintenance. When people work together in the shared maintenance of common-pool resources, they explore different ways of being with one another through collective subjectivities.

Related to this notion of care is Kathleen Fitzpatrick's exploration of "generous thinking" in the university, a mode of engagement that, Fitzpatrick writes, "emphasizes listening over speaking, community over individualism, and lingering with the ideas that are in front of us rather than pressing forward to where we want to go."[57] There is, then, an epistemological connotation to care that encourages us to maintain an openness to possible ways of knowing and to prioritise receptivity rather than end-directed rationality in our scholarly interactions. Conceived in this way, "open" can refer to an affective quality rather than a particular definitional state (open vs. closed). This kind of epistemic openness is explored by Stephen Pinfield in his book *Achieving Global Open Access*, where he argues for an approach to openness in which "different kinds of knowledge and knowledge systems are valued and engaged with across and beyond conventional science."[58] For Pinfield, an ethical approach to open access also requires epistemic openness and participatory openness to enable interactions between diverse communities. Both Fitzpatrick and Pinfield are arguing that the affectivity inherent within knowledge production requires a certain conception of the university and publishing—which I consider to be a kind of care.

María Puig de la Bellacasa further complicates Tronto and Fisher's definition of care to move beyond their focus on the human and to encompass the nonhuman, too, in order to conceive of "commitment and obligation as nonnormative forms of ethical engagement that could be more attuned to the decentering of human agency and privilege."[59] This includes considering "objects, things, and other than human animals, organisms, and forms as political in their very ontology." Though Puig de la Bellacasa's focus here is on ecological concerns, the importance of caring for nonhuman objects is also relevant for a book on publishing. Publishing is an issue of materiality, both digital and physical: books and articles exist within a web of relations that require care and attention for their creation, distribution, and preservation. This book therefore explores the relationship between OA and care in the policy arena and alternative approaches to publishing.

Importantly, however, the ethics of care is a question posed rather than an answer given; it is nonnormative rather than prescriptive of a way forward. This book is guided by a theoretical commitment to caring and to exploring how care relates to new forms of open access publishing. It is important, then, to not venerate care or assume that it is a panacea for all the ills of marketisation within publishing. Instead, I argue that care is not currently a particular concern of marketized forms of publishing but should be an important consideration in any emancipatory forms of OA publishing—how best to care for the multitude of possible relations and situations within the move to open access publishing?

Entanglement

Strongly related to care is the notion of entanglement, another methodological concern for this book. Aside from objective and detached forms of analysis, I am wholly entangled in the transition to open access and a firm advocate for collectivising approaches to publishing. This means that the empirical analysis and examples put forward here are not neutrally presented or even necessarily consistent with one another. They simply aim to explore the possibilities of a publishing that is answerable to actors beyond the market. This means caring not just for the situatedness of publishing, but for my own entanglements within it. Following Donna Haraway, this approach aims to "stay with the trouble" of the open access movement in order to make a "critical and joyful fuss about these matters."[60] It means accepting my embeddedness within various publishing communities—acknowledging that I am an advocate of certain open access practices—and thinking with these communities to explore the possibilities of collectivity within open access. For Haraway, again arguing from an ecologically minded perspective, staying with the trouble involves following different threads to create narratives about the issue at hand. This means paying attention to the worlds we build through our analysis, the actors we foreground, and the communities we represent—or as Haraway writes, "it matters what stories we tell to tell other stories with."[61]

The stories presented in this book intend to speak to this commitment to entanglement. I am, for example, drawing heavily on my own experience as co-organiser of the Radical Open Access Collective (ROAC), an organisation of more than eighty open access presses, journals, and other projects all run by working academics.[62] Much of the argument I make in chapters 3 and 4 is based on the working practices and forms of collaboration I have both witnessed and attempted to nurture through my activities with the ROAC. But my work with the ROAC also reveals the shortcomings and difficulties associated with collaboration, such as the fact that scholar-led publishers are too busy to fully commit to alternative forms of organisation, or the labour issues associated with DIY and grassroots publishing projects. I try to bring these issues to bear on the debate on OA by telling stories about the projects I have worked with. This requires acknowledgement of (and care for) my own entanglement with different open access projects.

I therefore aim to proceed carefully in the following chapters and will strive to appreciate the power relations and forms of mediation that exist between the human and nonhuman actors that influence the power of OA as a commons. This is achieved by both assembling actors and interpreting discursive statements that pertain to the sites analysed, using a variety of stories to do so. Such an approach will entail both articulating and composing certain realities—through my own entanglement with the material presented—in a care-full and responsible way.

Overview of the Book

The transition to open access embodies a range of ethico-political values and preconceptions held by the different actors involved in publishing. It also reflects the standards and values of a variety of institutional arrangements within libraries, research communities, funders, publishers, and the university more broadly. Taking care of this complexity, the book explores how OA can be reoriented away from market-centric practices and towards a commons mode of production. The following five chapters engage with policy-based and scholar-led interventions into open access and infrastructural governance in order to explore a variety of ways that commonality can be encouraged in publishing.

Chapter 1 establishes what is meant by the term *commons* and how it relates to open access publishing. It begins by discussing a handful of projects related to open access that utilise the term "commons"—Elsevier's "Digital Commons," FORCE11 Scholarly Commons Working Group, and the Creative Commons organisation—to understand how it is currently being deployed relative to open access. Through a discussion of these three projects, the chapter shows the range of practices on display in the deployment of the term "the commons" and their disparate politics and different meanings, particularly how many projects intend to evoke the language of participatory and freely accessible resources. Here, I caution against usages of the commons that do not attend to the forms of production inherent in creating these resources, showing how a fuller understanding of the commons requires appreciating who is creating and maintaining these common-pool resources (the commoners) and how they do so through practices of mutual reliance and care (commoning).

Based on this understanding of the commons mode of production, chapter 2 assesses Plan S, the governmental funder policy that seeks to mandate open access to all funded research in Europe, for its potential to promote collectivity and collaboration within OA publishing. Plan S represents a multifunder intervention into the market that seeks to promote a collaborative and equitable approach to freely accessible publications funded by public money, though it is not an overtly defined commons-based approach.[63] Plan S is billed as radical: it goes further than the majority of OA policies in its stated aims of engaging with the negative elements of the market practices of traditional publishers, rather than simply requiring free access to research articles in accordance with publisher demands. The policy mandates specific and somewhat onerous conditions from publishers and researchers that, I argue, amount to an attempted intervention into the market practices of the publishing industry.

Much has been written about Plan S, both by the architects of the policy and by those affected. This has included a public consultation that received hundreds of responses from different actors across the globe, itself a form of collective engagement (or at least a perceived form). The chapter assesses the politics of the policy's creation by critically analysing public statements from policymakers and their strategies of getting actors on board with the policy. Through the analysis, we see the tensions inherent within large-scale, maximalist approaches to OA that have radical ambitions to intervene in the market. On the one hand, the policymakers' rhetoric about making publishing more accountable to research communities is strong and persuasive, but on the other hand, their ability to intervene into this market is limited due to pervasive neoliberal governmentality that forces funders to prioritise market outcomes in their policymaking.

From the perspective of commons approaches to OA that promote collectivity and mutual reliance, we see the importance of prioritising, and not neglecting, locality in OA policymaking. Publishing is an inherently situated activity that is highly specific to individual disciplinary communities. Researchers feel strongly about their academic freedom to publish how they see fit, so interventions into local contexts require great sensitivity. Through the analysis, we see attempts by policymakers to appear to be consensus-building and collaborative in their policies, though the question remains of how collaborative this approach to publishing beyond the market this really is.

While chapters 1 and 2 explore how the dominant forms of OA largely rehearse the values of neoliberalism and are ultimately impotent against the marketisation of publishing and higher education, chapter 3 develops an understanding of the commons that reflects the motivations and practices of scholar-led publishers acting against commerciality. Though the individual presses analysed do not all share the same values, the chapter draws out a number of overlapping themes from their stated motivations and publishing practices, such as experimentation, an ethics of care, noncommercial practice, and critique of the status quo. The chapter begins with a brief history of scholar-led publishing in early e-journals and their importance as part of the "prehistory" of open access movements. These presses are theorised in accordance with what Christopher Kelty terms "recursive publics" to illustrate their experimental practices and technical self-sufficiency.[64] In contrast to OA policies, which are more concerned with promoting neoliberal logics of choice and individual market participation, I argue that scholar-led presses can be understood as reflecting a commons-based practice that could be supported through a number of infrastructural projects to truly nurture a scholarly commons grounded in care.

Once latent commons-based practices have been "located" in chapter 3, chapter 4 turns to the emerging discussion of open infrastructures for scholarly communication to see how they might contribute to a commons-based ecosystem for scholarly communication. The chapter discusses a number of initiatives founded to devise open-source infrastructures to support open access publishing, including the Radical Open Access Collective, the Community-led Open Publication Infrastructures for Monographs (COPIM) Project, and open-infrastructure projects in Latin America. It situates these projects within the commons framework described so far and explores how they might nurture the commons through self-governance and mutual reliance for publishing. The chapter considers how infrastructure and formalised governance systems may influence subjectivities in the commons, especially how they may create new forms of community and resilience, and care-full ways of being within higher education. Engaging with Massimo De Angelis's work on "boundary commoning" and projects that reflect this approach, the chapter describes how small but interlinked publishing projects may work together while still maintaining their individual autonomy. The COPIM project, for example, is theorised as reflecting this approach. Members of this organisation support one another by sharing resources/expertise and embedding each other's values within each project, what is termed "scaling small." This chapter is describing a novel approach to publishing infrastructure that foregrounds an ethic of care as the dominant logic of organisation. By exploring these new collaborative and open forms of self-governance, the approach described in chapter 4 also seeks to embed the values of care within university presses, library-led publishers, and a range of other organisations for academic publishing.

The book concludes by strategising around how to reorient publishing away from a focus on mere open access—i.e., openness to the outputs of publishing—and towards a richer commons-based discussion that prioritises self-organisation as a mode of production. In doing this, I argue that it is perhaps time to leave behind discussions of open access if we are to take seriously a more emancipatory understanding of the knowledge commons. I explore a variety of potential avenues for better community governance of higher education, including through editorial boards, learned societies, and research assessment reform, all which may in their own ways resist marketisation. The chapter makes an appeal for research communities to rethink their relationship with publishing, including with respect to career progression, precarious labour, and the overall understanding of what a university should be.

By this stage, the book will have also speculated a great deal about new forms of commoner subjectivity that could be brought about by the move to commons-based forms of publishing and new ways of being with one another. The concluding chapter explores how forms of mutual reliance and care may extend into other areas of the university too. It should now be clear that the commons I am arguing for is not a linear transition from one system of publishing to another. Rather, it is a way of embedding a multitude of care-based interventions into higher education so as to ultimately affect university culture more generally. The intent of the book is therefore to show how open access might be reconceived as a commons in a way that could be transformational for a number of different practices within neoliberal higher education.

Chapter 1

What Is the Relationship between Open Access Publishing and the Commons?

In 2017, the academic publisher Elsevier purchased a publishing and technology company called bepress.[1] For Elsevier, bepress represented a key component in their push for the technology to provide users with an end-to-end publishing system from preprints to journals, repositories, metrics, and beyond. Much of the value of bepress is based on its Digital Commons software, a cloud-based repository management system to which many North American university libraries subscribe to provide access to faculty journals and associated publications. Digital Commons allows libraries to host journals—both subscription and open access—and track metrics on faculty publications, representing a showcase of an institution's academic work.

Immediately after the acquisition was announced, many customers of bepress (previously an independent commercial organisation operating out of Berkeley, California) expressed dismay that Elsevier had purchased a company so embedded in library publishing and noncommercial open access. A website titled "Operation beprexit" was launched for universities to signal that they would discontinue their bepress contracts and seek alternative providers. Explaining Penn Libraries decision to leave bepress, Sara Leavens wrote:

> In August, bepress sold their company to Elsevier, a business with a history of aggressive confidentiality agreements, steep price increases, and opaque data mining practices. In their acquisition of bepress and other companies like SSRN and Mendeley, Elsevier demonstrates a move toward the consolidation and monopolization of products and services impacting all areas of the research lifecycle. We are worried about the long-term impacts from these acquisitions and are concerned that such changes are not in the best interests of the library community. Therefore, we feel obligated to begin exploring alternatives.[2]

The commercial practices of Elsevier are in large part responsible for the open access movement, which grew particularly in response to the "steep price increases" that Leavens cites, leading many researchers to officially boycott the publisher.[3] Many librarians feared that by buying a key component of library purchasing software, bepress would simply be reoriented to reflect the extractive, all-consuming approach of Elsevier more generally.

At the heart of this discussion is a product called Digital Commons, a service that allows universities to manage and share digital publications. Much like bepress, many products and services invoke the term "commons" to refer to resources shared freely with the public: Wikimedia Commons is an online collection of openly licensed and public-domain images and other cultural resources; Review Commons is a collection of freely accessible peer review reports; and Elsevier's Digital Commons is an institutional repository of freely accessible publications. Though the term "commons" is not defined by these organisations, there is a clear association between the term "commons" and the fact that they are making something freely available (review reports, publications, images, etc.). It is a term that resonates well with the push for open access and free culture, connoting a feel-good way of working that stands outside capitalist relations.

I am exploring in this book whether the commons represents an alternative possibility for open access, something able to help wrest control of scholarly communication away from commercial publishing and towards a scholar-governed future. But to do this, it is necessary to understand what the commons actually is and how there are different conceptions of it, particularly the differences between the commons as a *resource* and a *mode of production*. How, then, does the understanding of the commons deployed in this book differ from, for example, Elsevier's Digital Commons? Are they both commons-based approaches, or is Elsevier merely embarking on a strategy of "commons washing" to associate their product with participatory and collectivising publishing infrastructures?[4] This chapter cuts through the various understandings of the commons that relate to open access publishing and offers a richer definition than mere freely accessible resources.

The Commons and Common Resources

It is important to understand first that commons do concern resources, which is to say some form of shared physical or digital *thing* or collection of things. In ancient Rome, the term *res communis* was used to designate natural resources such as air and the seas, those naturally occurring forms of property that were shared by everyone. *Res communis* was in distinction to *res publicae*, or property owned by citizens and managed by the state, such as highways or navigable rivers.[5] Further on in history, "the commons" is identifiable within English medieval life as a form of land management and usage by local villagers on feudal manors. Locals did not own common land, but landowners granted them rights to graze livestock in exchange for returning produce to the lords of the manor as rent.[6] So, commons relate to resources shared between, or "common to," groups of people. But to whom are these resources common, and how does this relate to open access publishing? We can explore this question with respect to the licences produced by the Creative Commons organisation.

Creative Commons (CC) licenses are addenda to traditional copyright that grant blanket permissions to digital works, allowing licensors to keep their copyright and attribution rights while stipulating how a work may be reused (for commercial purposes, for use in another derivative work, etc.) The most permissive CC licence, Creative Commons attribution (CC BY), is stipulated by many as the way to achieve true open access, an argument made by signatories of canonical definitions of open access such as the BOAI declaration.[7] CC-licensed academic works are openly accessible because they allow free sharing and reuse without explicit permission from the original author. Thousands of academic works are released under Creative Commons, and public and private funders around the world require use of the licences in their policies. The Wellcome Trust, for example, claims:

> We believe that the full research and economic benefit of published content will only be realised when there are no restrictions on access to, and re-use of, this information. In our view this is best achieved through the use of the internationally recognised CC BY licence.[8]

In an academic context, CC licences are not only about making work freely available to read; they also aim to reduce the kinds of friction that copyright restrictions lead to when authors want to reuse figures, text, and tables in their articles. The licences themselves offer blanket permission to allow people to reuse work, while still requiring reusers to cite the original author as the creator of the piece.

Creative Commons reflects a resource-based definition of the commons in that it is unconcerned with the forms of production that went into creating the resources. Anything can be part of the Creative Commons providing it is shared according to a licence that grants certain permissions for sharing and reuse by anyone. CC's understanding of the commons is thus akin to a public domain whereby resources are freely available to everyone (albeit with certain restrictions). In 2001, Lawrence Lessig, one of the founders of Creative Commons, discussed the commons in his book *The Future of Ideas: The Fate of the Commons.*[9] Here, Lessig argues that a variety of different resources are "commons," from public streets to writings in the public domain, primarily because they are "free for others to take."[10] CC-licensed works are common resources, according to this definition, because they are also free for others to take.

Digital articles are freely shareable without depriving others of access: one person can share a digital file with another and they will both have access to that file. They are what economists would term "nonrivalrous" because their usage does not lead to their depletion.[11] This is in distinction to rivalrous resources, such as forests, fisheries, reservoirs, etc., that do deplete when used. Though both rivalrous and nonrivalrous resources can be managed according to commons principles, open access publishing has traditionally been associated with the power of digital resources to permit unlimited sharing.[12] Networked digital technologies, which can share nonrivalrous resources at a fraction of the cost of physical books and journals, are the foundation of the digital, resource-based understanding of the commons.

Creative Commons, and its ideology of a digital commons filled with freely accessible resources, fits well with the ideology of Silicon Valley that has dominated technology since the 1990s. CC is resolutely probusiness and individualistic, employing talk of progressive politics while restating the values of neoliberal capitalism. Lessig, in his book on free culture, writes: "[the] free culture I defend in this book is a balance between anarchy and control. A free culture, like a free market, is filled with property. It is filled with rules of property and contract that get enforced by the state."[13] Lessig positions CC-licenced resources as operating within a capitalist economy that uses free culture to enhance and improve the business prospects of those who share. This is why Creative Commons sees itself as promoting "innovation" and "reach and impact" alongside participation and uniting around an undefined "common cause."[14] This commitment to liberal individualism is not only reflected in the attribution requirement for CC-licensed works, which individualises the work as the sole property of its creator, but it is also noticeable in much of Creative Commons's framing of the benefits of CC licensing to the *creators*. For example, they write: "the fact that the name of the creator follows a CC-licensed work makes the licenses an important means to develop a reputation or, in corporate speak, a brand."[15] Creative Commons therefore utilises the language of progressive politics mixed with the business-friendly hallmarks of branding and innovation.

From this perspective, CC's understanding of the commons is something of a liberal political imaginary buoyed by the promise of freely accessible digital resources created through market mechanisms and digital entrepreneurialism. This understanding of the commons is akin to a somewhat diluted public domain in which resources are free to access with certain reuse rights, all while remaining the property of the original creator, the individual proprietorial subject. As Gary Hall writes: "Contrary to the way Creative Commons is frequently portrayed, then, it is not advocating a common stock of nonprivately owned (creative) works that everyone jointly manages, shares, and is free to access and use on the same basis at all, which is how the Commons is often understood."[16] CC licences reinforce creative and academic works as the property of the individual author or creator, who then grants certain permissions for reuse to all users without exclusion.

Other resource-based understandings of the commons go further than CC's liberal project by advocating for a "common stock" of property owned by *all* and not just the creator in question. For example, in their book *Commonwealth*, Hardt and Negri understand the commons along left lines as something literally owned by all. In addition to the commonwealth of natural resources, the authors argue for common ownership of the "results of social production that are necessary for social interaction and further production, such as knowledges, languages, codes, information, affects, and so forth."[17] Such an understanding goes further than Creative Commons by advocating for common (rather than individualistic) property of resources, eschewing the notion of private property altogether. In this sense, from the perspective of open access publishing, digital texts would form part of an ecosystem of digital and physical resources that would be owned by and common to everyone. While I am certainly more sympathetic to this view, Hardt and Negri's understanding of the commons once again emphasises the resources that can be used and reused (and are owned) by all, as opposed to the forms of production created and maintained by and for specific communities of people.

So, there are resource-based understandings of the commons that arise from different political perspectives, though all influence open access publishing in a similar way. In either instance, the commons is considered a kind of public domain in which resources (publications, for our purposes) are made freely available to all. This means that such understandings start from the premise of the commons as a place of freely accessible resources for all, rather than a mode of production or institutional arrangement for communities that manage their resources (as others do). This resource-based understanding is primarily how the commons is deployed within advocacy for open access publishing, to which the quotations above from Lessig and the Creative Commons organisation and others attest. Because of its close association with Creative Commons licences, it is easy to see why there is such a strong understanding of the open access publishing commons as about nothing more than publicly available publications.

Yet to fully understand what Creative Commons was trying to achieve, it is also worth situating Lessig's liberal arguments in favour of the commons against the backdrop of the legal scholarship milieu in the postdigital age. The digital revolution brought with it an optimism associated with networked technologies and their ability to share nonrivalrous resources more efficiently, at zero marginal cost and, crucially, without the need for individual ownership of these files. The legal scholar James Boyle wrote in 2008 how the expansion of nonrivalrous digital materials has led the state to inappropriately extend individual property rights to these resources—when they are better considered a public domain. Boyle terms this process the "second enclosure movement," referencing the original enclosure movement that led to the denial of peasant rights to common land on which they depended to survive.[18] The second enclosure movement, Boyle argues, stacks intellectual property rights to digital material firmly in favour of the companies who initially produced them. Digital enclosure, therefore, presents a barrier to a competitive market through the unnecessary friction it adds to processes of distribution, innovation, and transaction. A better approach, he claims, is the digital commons.

Boyle uses the terms "commons" and "public domain" interchangeably, writing "some would say it is a commons only if the whole of society has access to it. This is the view I take here."[19] The "it" here is the digital object—not the way in which it is produced—and so the commons is equivalent to a global public resource to which we all have access to use in certain ways, rather than something with more local significance. Boyle's work is situated in a rich tradition of liberal scholarship that advocates for the public domain in the face of perceived monopolisation of intellectual property. For Boyle, the public domain is a tool for stimulating creativity, scientific endeavour, and democracy, and especially market interaction. He writes: "the more commodified and restricted our access to information, the less efficient the operation of the market, the more poorly it allocates resources in our society."[20] The public domain of resources provides the building blocks of this liberal democratic society. The commons, then, is a means to the end of a more efficient market for allocating resources, moving us towards the "perfect information" that is the defining feature of a "perfect market."[21]

While I disagree with this understanding of the commons as *a public domain of resources*, I do think it is worth taking the work of Boyle and Lessig and others seriously in the context in which they were writing. Elevating the public domain above more traditional individualistic forms of intellectual property is a worthy cause, and Creative Commons has done much to contribute to this cultural catalogue of available material. Yet it also reflects an understanding of the world that elides the ways in which resources are produced, maintained, and shared according to a specific political-economic logic. I would like to suggest here that the understanding of the commons as primarily a freely accessible resource (or collection of resources) is both limiting in its application to open access publishing and elides important work that positions the commons as concerning *resource creation and/or management by specific communities*, rather than purely or even necessarily about granting free access for all of society. It is vital to consider these alternative conceptions for their ability to shed light on a different and more politicised understanding of open access publishing that prioritises the commons as a mode of producing shared resources, the rules/norms for maintaining them, and a way of relating around shared resources. This will reveal a fuller and more nuanced understanding of the benefits of the commons for open access publishing.

Commons, Market, and State

Conceiving of the commons as a (mere) space of freely accessible resources is insufficient for a full picture because it fails to account for the ways these resources are produced. A richer definition would move beyond the commons as a political imaginary of freely shared resources and towards the promotion of community-based organisation and production over the state and the market. As Carlo Vercellone explains, the commons "cannot be ascribed to the intrinsic nature of goods, but to the ability of labour to self-organise."[22] This means that the commons is about self-organisation, governance, and the rules and maintenance for creating and maintaining these resources. For Vercellone, the commons requires the "establishment of a new hierarchy between Common, private and public" that shuns the simple divide between market and state and illustrates how self-organisation has the ability to complicate public and private modes of production.[23] This is not to position the commons as outside or separate from the market or the state, because it is always already implicated in each mode of production; rather, it is to foreground community self-organisation as integral to any approach to the commons.

The commons in this sense is highly relevant to scholarly publishing, which has been increasingly marketised since the 1980s.[24] Open access was in part motivated in response to the egregious market practices of large commercial publishers, most notably Elsevier, Wiley, Springer Nature, and Taylor & Francis. With a handful of large, high-profit commercial publishers controlling much of journal publishing, the industry has been described as oligopolistic due to its consolidated nature.[25] These publishers continue to make sizeable returns from the sale of journal subscriptions to libraries, the price of which has outstripped inflation since the mid-1990s.[26] By freeing access to journal articles through cheaper digital distribution mechanisms, many arguments for OA have sought to replace the toll-access system of publishing with an open access system funded through a range of business models, albeit one in which the profit margins of the big publishers are reduced.[27]

However, for the most part, open access has allowed large commercial publishers to consolidate their market power through an additional revenue stream alongside their already profitable journal subscriptions, most notably through the popularity of article-processing charges in which authors pay a fee for publication, but also through the increasingly popular publishing agreements that bundle the cost of reading together with the cost of publishing. Much like with subscriptions, APCs and publishing agreements have been a hugely successful model for large commercial publishers, with six publishers taking over half of reported article-processing-charge revenues.[28] If open access intended to lower the profits of commercial publishers, it does not seem to have succeeded. Publishing continues to be a predominantly marketized industry controlled by private entities, rather than one operating in the service of the public or common good.

So despite the fact that much academic research is funded by taxpayer money, and that editorial labour and content are provided for free by working academics, publishing is still largely controlled by market forces and the financial returns are privatised. This means that the hierarchy between the market, the state, and the commons is strongly weighted towards the market, in accordance with the global trend of neoliberalisation over the past four decades that has weakened the state and elevated private industry as the preferred method of control and organisation. It is here that the commons as a mode of production based on self-organisation is useful as a counterpoint. Rather than defining the commons based purely on resources, as Creative Commons does, for example, a more appropriate understanding for open access publishing would focus on the forms of organisation and community governance for creating, maintaining, and sharing these resources.

The Nobel Prize–winning economist Elinor Ostrom dedicated her career to the study of commons, which she and Charlotte Hess define as "a resource shared by a group of people that is subject to social dilemmas."[29] Though this definition preserves the importance of resources, it is the "social dilemmas" that are most interesting from Ostrom's perspective—namely, how local communities may coalesce around a shared resource through rules, community norms, and dispute-resolution mechanisms. Ostrom primarily studied natural commons—fisheries, water supplies, etc.—to understand why some common-pool resources are successfully managed while others become depleted or riven by conflict. The success of common-pool governance is down to a range of factors such as the kind of resource, its size, the actors involved in maintenance, institutional arrangements, and so on. Once seen in this light, it is clear that the commons is less about freely accessible resources and more about organisation and production.

From the perspective of publishing, the infrastructures, journals, and other associated publications are complex sociotechnical resources that are also subject to social dilemmas. They comprise physical and digital components, managed by a variety of stakeholder actors, and are not created solely for or by market-centric forces of production. For example, academic journals are led by academic editors, reviewers, and authors, administered by publishers, organised by librarians, and have a variety of constituent audiences. For Potts and colleagues, academic journals are "club goods," i.e., "non-market solutions to public-good problems that rely on the ability of self-constituted groups both to self-organise and successfully to self-govern."[30] This means that they usually entail rules, membership processes, and ways of excluding certain actors, informal or otherwise.

For Potts et al., a journal is not a private good that exists solely to make profit, nor is it a public good that can be enjoyed and sustained by whoever wants to contribute. Instead, it is a club good that provides a "formation of groups of people who share a common concern, who are willing to pool their common resources and specialisation-skills, and to act in concert in pursuit of 'shared externalities.'"[31] This means that a journal necessarily entails exclusion and some form of locality (not necessarily geographical, but disciplinary or another community-uniting factor). For these reasons, Potts et al. argue, the economics of club goods "overlap substantially" with the economics of knowledge commons, which also concern local communities self-organising to produce and maintain their resources. In the quest to reclaim publishing from the market, locality is one key feature to be elevated over publisher-led economies of scale that dehumanise publishing through automation and de-localise it through homogenising tech-led models.

Yet many explicit attempts to position scholarly communication as a commons fail to adequately consider locality as one of the defining features of the commons-based form of production. Instead, terms such as "global commons" are utilised to refer to the collective management of scholarly communication by and for a global population.[32] For Heather Morrison, the knowledge commons is "a system where the world's scholarly knowledge is available to everyone, everywhere, to draw from and contribute to, one that prioritizes the values and needs of scholars, scholarship, and the public good, and is open to all by default."[33] Many advocates of an open-access commons speak about an "overall transition of the scholarly publishing system" from a global, toll-access system to a freely accessible one, taking a holistic and maximalist standpoint that again reinforces the commons as a freely accessible collection of resources.[34]

One notable attempt to advocate for a commons-based approach to open access is the FORCE Scholarly Commons Working Group, in which Bosman et al. propose the digital scholarly commons as a way to ensure that new initiatives for scholarly communication form a coherent and interoperable system that acts as a viable alternative to traditional modes of publishing. The authors argue for "a set of principles and rules for the community of researchers and other stakeholders to subscribe to, the practices based on those principles, and the common pool of resources around which the principles and practices evolve."[35] Such principles are intended to create an "agreement among knowledge producers and users." The authors set out to define a set of principles that are designed to be inclusive to stakeholders in all disciplines, both commercial and noncommercial providers, and all forms of scholarly output from papers to data to code:

1. Research and knowledge should be freely available to all who wish to use or reuse it.
2. Participation in the production and use of knowledge should be open to all who wish to participate.
3. There should be no systemic barriers and disincentives to prevent either such free use or open participation.[36]

These principles are accompanied by a set of rules participants should follow in order to maintain the commons. The basis of this idea is that the commons should be open to all and governed according to principles that do not prohibit access or participation. If organisations decline to follow these principles, then they cannot be considered part of the commons.

While this approach avoids the trappings of being focused merely on resources (as per Creative Commons above), it is ultimately inadequate due to its indiscriminate approach to governance, which lacks local context and invites commercial organisations back into the fold. Unlike Potts et al., the FORCE approach positions the commons as more of a global public good than something shared locally. Yet the whole point of the commons is community self-organisation and management, and so principles and rules cannot be deduced from a neutral or global perspective that affects everyone the same way. So, rather than implying a free-for-all, as advocates of a global commons may argue, the commons I am arguing for requires or entails exclusion, often along community lines. This means that some people have the right to access, use, or maintain a resource, whereas others do not (though barriers are often fuzzy); they also have the rights to democratically set and implement the rules within their community. These people are called "commoners."

The term "commoners" evokes those who dwelled on and maintained the common land owned by the lords of the manor under feudal rule (particularly in England). Locals were granted access to common lands to graze livestock (pannage/herbage), collect wood (estovers), or take peat or turf (turbary), all in exchange for certain taxes paid to the lord. Local commoners were granted strips of land for growing food; decisions regarding harvest were made collectively and democratically by all within the commons. Harvests were shared and rules were in place to ensure that no one took more than their fair allocation. Common-land management is evidence of communal resource allocation through mutual reliance. However, the commons should not be valorised as a perfect mode of production, isolated from all external influences. Silvia Federici illustrates how, contrary to naive historical understandings that portray feudal society as harmonious, the medieval village was actually a "theater of daily warfare."[37] Lords would try to limit peasant access to common land through litigation, taxation, and demands that peasants carry out certain "labour services" on the lord's land.[38] Jean Birrell describes how in the thirteenth and early fourteenth centuries lords were continually litigating against commoners for using more of the commons than laws permitted, despite the fact that "the erosion of pastures and woodland inevitably reduced the area in which [common rights] could be exercised, while the number of commoners increased."[39] The increase in population size, in addition to a loss of common land, meant commoners were forced to share less common land with more commoners. This struggle was to continue through to the modern period, when it was made worse by the dissolution of the monasteries in the sixteenth century, which resulted in the enclosure and commodification of large swathes of common land.[40]

More contemporary perspectives, like those of the late theorist José Esteban Muñoz, continue to emphasise both endogenous and exogenous conflict within the commons. For Muñoz, the "turbulence" of life in the commons is necessary because of both the continuous threats of enclosure and the disagreement and plurality within the commons. The world is not primarily designed for common ways of working and belonging, continually pitting commoners against one another, and against the outside, meaning that finding a way to work together in common is a continuous uphill struggle. Yet crucially, Muñoz claims, this disharmony is the very thing that gives the commons its "insurrectionist promise."[41] If common life were entirely placid, communities would stagnate and homogenise, smoothing over the possibilities that difference offers and reverting to traditional hierarchical arrangements.

From the perspective of academic publishing, I too am at pains to emphasise that the commons is not a harmonious mode of production within individual communities, even those that appear entirely consensual. There is antagonism and conflict, and disputes need adequate resolution mechanisms that allow "participants to air differences and to achieve resolutions that they consider legitimate, fair, and scientifically sound," as Hess and Ostrom emphasise.[42] Rules and processes therefore need to be designed by participants, and each resource will necessitate a different set of rules or norms: there is no straightforward roadmap for commons-based resource production; each is unique. For the commons method of production to be applicable to publishing, locality and difference must be embedded from the start, such as different publishing cultures, career levels, or institutional arrangements. The move to OA publishing allows us to work out the best institutional arrangements and governance procedures for communities to engage in inclusive, nonmarketised systems of publishing. This means starting from a position that knowledge production is localised and heterogenous and should therefore be about supporting diverse communities to do their work.

By this stage, it should be clear that much of the discourse on the commons and OA publishing lacks nuance, depth, or applicability to a range of local contexts. By moving away from a purely resource-based understanding of the commons, and eschewing a global, homogenising approach that fails to consider local contexts, we can see that the commons I am arguing for refers to a particular kind of self-organised production and governance, rather than a utopian form of research access. It is one in which the market and the state are modes of production subservient to self-organisation and community management (though not entirely absent). This conception, I maintain, is most useful for our ability to encourage the governance and control of scholarly communication by research communities themselves.

The Commons as Practice (Commoning)

If we take a tripartite approach to the commons mode of production, we see that it involves common-pool resources (the commons), people who share and maintain these resources (commoners), and, as I shall now describe, the practices of shared enterprise and mutual reliance that sustain the commons, termed "commoning." It is vital to consider all three of these features as relevant to any commons-based system of production, and it is particularly relevant for imagining commons that are emancipatory from traditional or marketised forms of publishing (and the hierarchies they entail). Commoning is perhaps the most important (but least explored) aspect of the commons because it reveals the possibility of new forms of relating together that are emancipatory from (neo)liberal individualism and competition.

The practices of commoning arise within a particular locality. They are not community rules, but rather are situated norms that revolve around the production and maintenance of a community resource, be it a housing cooperative, a free-software project, or a local community group.[43] Commoning is based on the premise that mutual reliance is necessary in cooperative enterprises because the community is entirely responsible for its own existence. For example, Patrick Bresnihan illustrates the practices of mutual reliance with the fisheries of Castletownbere in Ireland, in which fishermen share surplus catches with one another, guided by the principle of "I store my meat in the belly of my brother."[44] No one is legally required to share with another, but there is a strong community norm of doing so because of the recognition that commoners are all entangled with each other's survival and well-being. In this sense, the local community sustains itself through gift-giving and other forms of property- and labour-sharing that are alien to individuating modes of working.

Commoning, as Bresnihan argues, starts with the "immediate and intimate understanding that the world is *already shared*," in recognition of the entangled nature of subjectivity that is frequently denied in neoliberal societies.[45] From a similar standpoint, Fred Moten and Stefano Harney describe how "the commons cannot gather us. We are already gathered, as we are already dispersed and interspersed."[46] These understandings of subjectivity require us to consider the necessity of mutual reliance within shared spaces and the ways in which commoners are entangled with each other and their surroundings. Away from liberal theories of the rational, self-determined individual, the understanding of the commons as a practice of commoning can point to (and nurture) new forms of subjectivities that foreground cooperating collectives over competitive individuals. This means that commoning presents a different understanding of the subject as relationally dependent on the care of other commoners, in contrast to the neoliberal market-state dichotomy that positions the subject as productive and self-reliant. This is also why I locate care as an important practice within commons-based situations. Commoning is a form of care oriented around a specific resource.

When applied to OA, commoning has emancipatory potential for academic publishing and the university more broadly. Much of this potential is currently speculative as a possibility, primarily because the university is a space of competition for scarce resources and a decreasing number of jobs, which works against collaboration and collectivity by pitting researchers against one another. Publishing is representative of competition in academia: scholars are required to be *productive* in their publishing routines, aiming to publish in prestigious publications to advance their careers, at the expense of other more collaborative endeavours. Though editorial decisions are, for the most part, made by academics (though market considerations are also important in the publication of books), ownership of the means of producing publications and the profits from journal subscriptions and book sales rests predominantly in private hands. This means that market-based publishing is extractive of academic labour and then privatises the gains.[47]

Yet it is precisely these conditions that commoning could help undermine and transform through an emphasis on cooperation between academics, librarians, publishers, and other actors involved in knowledge creation and dissemination. As Peter Suber notes, it is a "lucky accident" that academics receive no remuneration for authoring, editing, and reviewing:

> It's not a new fact of academic life, arising from a recent economic downturn in the publishing industry. Nor is it a case of corporate exploitation of unworldly academics. Scholarly journals haven't paid authors for their articles since the first scholarly journals, the *Philosophical Transactions* of the Royal Society of London and the *Journal des sçavans*, launched in London and Paris in 1665.[48]

For Suber, this historical quirk of academic publishing is one of the two main conditions for the possibility of open access (the other being the internet). The fact that academics provide the content and much of the editorial and production labour with no expectation of financial reward means that they would not lose anything by giving their publications away for free. Academics are in a position to argue for OA publishing, Suber claims, because they only stand to gain from better distribution of their work through OA.

While there is merit to this argument, a better way to view the unremunerated nature of scholarly publishing is through the promise of control. Academics control much of the labour for publishing; collectively, they prop up the entire industry for symbolic, rather than financial, capital through prestige and service work. Rather than viewing this situation as a bargaining chip to force publishers into open access, a more impactful way of understanding the relationship between publisher and academic would be that it affords the possibility for academics to demand control of the publishing process itself. It is through commoning that this is possible.

Commoning, as commons theorist Massimo De Angelis shows, does not take place only within a particular commons-based mode of production; it also occurs within capitalist enterprise in the form of reliance between workers, who care for one another and share knowledge, although it is a practice from which capitalism extracts.[49] Think about the ways you relate to your colleagues, look after them, and deeply understand their ways of working (for better or worse!)—these relationships are all grounded on a kind of care that is exploited by commercial organisations, but still has radical potential. Practices of care such as this illustrate the emancipatory potential of commoning from, in our case, private and marketized forms of publishing in which academics provide the labour in a form of commoning that is commodified as part of journal subscriptions and book sales. For De Angelis, these kinds of labour issues are exactly where commoning is most important; he writes, "[T]he key issue is not really how we conceive of commoning within the spheres of commons, but how we reclaim the commons of our production that are distorted through the imposition of capital's measure of things."[50] The task of an approach to publishing that is emancipatory from market control is to strategically withdraw the labour extracted by commercial publishers and redirect it to those who offer self-governance through the commons.

So, publishing resonates well with commoning because the unremunerated labour for the creation and maintenance of academic books and journals is a practice of mutual reliance through editorial care, community-building, and service to one's discipline. This means that much of the labour for academic publishing is not commodity-seeking, although it is routinely commodified by publishers in the sale of books and journals and, increasingly, processing charges for OA. Understanding the practices of commoning on display in traditional marketized forms of publishing is one way to recognise the possible transformation to greater scholar control that OA publishing *could* entail. For this reason, commoning points towards what J. K. Gibson-Graham et al. term a "postcapitalist politics"—a space to work through the inequities of capitalism and neoliberalism—that is located in the "shared present" and not some "elusive future."[51] Commoning is already an everyday practice in publishing, and often in higher education too, and just needs to be redirected to emancipatory ends.

"Commoning" the Movement for Open Access

Throughout this chapter, I have endeavoured to illustrate that the commons is relevant to OA publishing, but that it is routinely misapplied or ill-defined in OA advocacy. This is important because, as I have shown, the commons as a mode of production and practice holds great promise for forms of publishing that are not controlled by market values; they just need to be properly theorised. Understood as a hierarchy of market, state, and commons, the commons is not an either/or phenomenon; it is instead a mode of production that prioritises self-organisation while interacting with the state and the market in various ways through regulation, public funding, and the sale of services/resources, for example. Following David Fagundes, we can use the term "commonsiness" to describe the extent to which a project displays commons values by prioritising the self-organisation of labour for the purposes of shared enterprise.[52] Commonsiness reveals the ill-defined and messy nature of the commons and the practices of commoning, which often lie hidden in plain sight. The term helps communicate the complicated relationship of the commons to market and state forms of production that is necessarily implicated with each but not dominated by either.

Returning to the initial example of Digital Commons, it is clear that Elsevier's software has a complicated relationship with the various components that comprise the commons. Taking a liberal, resource-based understanding of the commons like the one employed by the Creative Commons organisation, it is possible to theorise Digital Commons as a commons because it offers open access resources to the public (though by no means all publications are publicly accessible through Digital Commons). This resource-based understanding of the commons is probably how the software acquired its name. Digital Commons would therefore fit neatly with the kind of commons that Lessig describes, and with the Silicon Valley understanding of the commons that favours a digital public domain that does not seek to question the commercial forces that created it.

Yet by looking at bepress from the perspective of the tripartite definition of common resources, commoners, and commoning, a more complicated picture emerges. Based on this understanding, forms of commoning may be at play between academic journal editors, reviewers, and authors that are facilitated by Digital Commons (as per any other academic journal). There may also be a sense of locality in particular library-based publishing programmes, and the publications may be produced and held in common to all. However, the hierarchy between the market, the state, and the commons is strongly weighted towards the market, because the value is captured by Elsevier and the overall governance of the software rests with its developers. This means that the users of Digital Commons cannot self-govern, but are instead beholden to a market player that extracts the labour of academics. Private, market actors are the primary governing forces for those using Digital Commons, and so the academic community has little say about how the software is used, its design, and the rules around maintaining it. From this perspective, Elsevier's Digital Commons represents a kind of "commons washing," as Dulong Rosnay writes:

> Such appropriations [of the commons] lead to new forms of "enclosure" of common resources, as private actors come to dominate the governance structures for the commons-based production of a good, or the provision of a service, thereby perverting key features and values of commons-based production, [a form of takeover] that happens with the private actor pretending to work for the commons, or at least using its semantics.[53]

So, the separate lineages of "the commons" allow it to be captured by market actors who seek to profit from their products and services. The term offers an association with participatory or self-governed forms of production, even where it simply refers to a freely accessible resource that is still the ultimate intellectual property of its creator.

The different conceptions of the commons explored in this chapter illustrate both its malleability and its potential. Though the term is routinely deployed in OA advocacy as the telos of the OA movement, a harmonious state in which all the world's knowledge is freely shared, it is rarely interrogated as a form of production that might help return *control* of academic publishing to researchers and the university more broadly. But a focus on governance and self-organisation would allow the reorientation of the OA movement from its focus on freely accessible outputs to one on equitable cultures of knowledge production away from market governance.

OA publishing has not yet reined in the marketisation of publishing, even though market practices were one of the major motivations for the movement and continue to be a strong theme in calls for open access.[54] Instead, publishers have successfully monetised open access through a range of new models, including the much-maligned article-processing charge, all while continuing to charge for journal subscriptions. It is also important to recognise that market efficiency was a key feature of the OA movement (itself not united in its aims), particularly from policymakers looking to return purchasing power to researchers and libraries in the form of article-processing charges.[55] This transitional state between OA and subscriptions, predicated on a commercial model of "hybrid" OA, has been termed the "worst of both worlds" because it allows large subscription publishers to increase their dominance of the publishing market.[56] The transition from a closed to an open publishing system looks certain to strengthen the publishing oligopoly rather than undermine its market dominance, especially as smaller publishers are bought up by larger ones in the hope of increasing the number of publications they can monetise.

But rather than seeing OA publishing as a transition from an inefficient closed system to an efficient open one, a better way to view it is through the commons lens described in this chapter, as a way of reclaiming control of scholarly communication through self-organised approaches to the governance, maintenance, and production of publishing. This is an intervention-based approach, rather than one grounded in systemic change from one system to another, in recognition of the fact that the commons is always already implicated with the forms of production from which it is said to be separate. So instead of considering OA publishing a transition from one marketised system of publishing to another, I argue throughout this book for reordering the hierarchy of market, state, and commons towards the commons, thus opening the space for postcapitalist publishing, policy, and infrastructure governed beyond mere market forces.

It is important to note that the commons does not imply specific rules around how a resource should be governed. I have tried to emphasise the importance of locality—the commoners who maintain the resource—and the undefined practices of commoning that arise spontaneously from cooperation and mutual reliance. This means I will not be presenting a blueprint or system of rules for how publishing should be governed, but rather an analysis of how, in various ways, certain market interventions may promote self-governance. As Carlo Vercellone notes, although nothing about a particular resource necessarily lends itself to a commons mode of governance, it is the resource itself and its local context that dictate how the rules should be established.[57] This process should be controlled by the community in question, and defining this community is a key dimension of the issue that must be continually reassessed. For Ostrom, too, the rules for a particular common resource are locally situated rather than given in advance, and her "Institutional Analysis and Diversity Framework" offers a way to understand the various elements that make up the commons in order to design adequate governance.[58] A fishery, for example, will be governed much differently than Wikipedia, but both will require dispute-resolution mechanisms, rules for contributing, and other forms of governance that can adapt to particular situations.

Using the understanding of the commons developed in this chapter, I now turn to Plan S, the European policy framework that seeks a joined-up cross-funder approach that mandates OA as a condition of grant funding. Though Plan S does not explicitly advocate a commons-based approach, it is does represent an attempt at a significant market intervention—a way to force commercial publishers to adopt certain practices—and is thus relevant for any analysis of ways of keeping the publishing market accountable. Yet Plan S is also top down, in that it imposes certain conditions on where and how researchers can publish, all while changing the business practices of academic publishers more generally. How will Plan S inhibit or enable certain common-based practices in publishing? Or will the status quo merely persist?

Chapter 2

Plan S

Careless Policy Interventions into the Publishing Market

Common strategies in the push for OA include the use of policies and mandates. Universities, funders, and governments use such policies to require open access to the research conducted by grantees and academic staff, which is achieved through both repositories (green OA) and journals or books (gold OA). Different conditions are attached around embargoes and CC licensing. The Registry of Open Access Repository Mandates and Policies has collected over a thousand of these policies, with more being added every month.[1] Having matured over the past decade, the OA policy landscape is heading towards a requirement for immediate OA as standard, but it remains flexible regarding routes to OA and licensing requirements. This means that both green and gold approaches are still common in OA policymaking (which often involves a mixture of both), while tolerance for an embargo period is being phased out by funders and other policymakers.

OA policies are a source of contention within the broader academic community and the publishing industry and reflect a struggle between different actors attempting to assert their power. Such policies are premised on the idea that external agencies—be they private or public—can to some extent determine how the research they fund is disseminated. In the case of government-funded research, one often-cited argument is that taxpayers should be able to access publicly funded research, as they have facilitated it, while private agencies often justify such mandates as part of their charitable missions.[2] Policies are controversial because they entail a perceived tradeoff between the individual's right to publish in whichever ways they feel necessary—sometimes cited as a condition of academic freedom[3]—and the collective benefits of greater public access to research. Yet in practice, academics already face many conditions around how and when to publish their work, especially due to the informal hierarchies of prestige that exist within academic publishing. OA mandates may be an additional burden on an already overstretched academic community, but they do not inhibit academic freedom in any real or meaningful sense.

I am writing in the UK, a country at the vanguard of OA policymaking that has invested huge sums into ensuring that all UK research is freely available. In 2012, the UK government-commissioned "Finch Report" was published. Led by Dame Janet Finch, the report's authors—comprising publishers, academics, librarians, and research funders—were tasked with working out how to "expand access" to UK research articles and "to propose a programme of action to that end."[4] Much of the UK government's move towards OA was instigated by David Willets, then Conservative Minister for Higher Education, who wrote passionately about his own book-writing experience as an independent researcher locked out of academic journal subscriptions simply because he did not have a university affiliation. For Willetts, OA allows us not only to reduce the inequities of research access, but to engage the broader public around academic research, and to act as a global showcase for UK research.[5] He was consequently interested in encouraging the publishing industry to shift business models from subscriptions to OA models, citing the impact of file sharing on the music industry and its need to find a web-based solution through companies like Spotify and Apple's iTunes, noting that "none of us want to see that fate overtake the publishing industry."[6]

In a lengthy report to Willetts, the authors of the Finch Report concluded that "a clear policy direction should be set towards support for publication in OA or hybrid journals, funded by APCs, as the main vehicle for the publication of research, especially when it is publicly funded."[7] Although APCs were not a new model in 2012, having been a common feature of biomedical publishing for a number of years, the Finch recommendation was to help normalise author payments for publishing, and it became a template for other national policymakers to copy. The Finch Report directly led to the introduction of the UK Research Council's (RCUK) OA policy, which required CC BY open access to all RCUK-funded research articles immediately on publication.[8] This policy also established a block grant distributed to universities for payment of OA fees (and associated costs) that still exists today. In subsequent years, as funders across the world made money available for fees, the article-processing charge became the dominant model for OA publishing. Many identify this model as illustrative of the iniquitous nature of OA: that it forces a "pay to say" culture onto academics, excludes researchers in disciplines and geographies that lack access to funding, and reorients academic publishing towards a low-quality, high-volume business model.[9]

Without wishing to attribute too much causation to these policy interventions, the RCUK policy and the Finch Report were unarguably important events in the development of OA policy and the resulting shift in publisher business models. As mentioned in the introduction to this book, this shift was grounded in a philosophy of marketisation that assumed researchers would become price-sensitive by choosing cheaper publishers in a way that would keep high prices in check. Indeed, the same logic had been applied by David Willetts just two years earlier when he increased undergraduate tuition fees in UK universities from £3,290 to £9,000 on the assumption that universities would compete for students by offering lower tuition fees (which of course never happened). Much of OA policy has therefore been driven by a free-market ideology based on the idea that rational individuals making self-interested choices will lead to better cultures of publishing than government regulation or other interventions.

It is important to keep this ideology in mind when analysing OA policy at the governmental level and seeking to understand whether and how radical ideas of the commons might fit into these dominant approaches to OA publishing. While Plan S, as this chapter discusses, initially presented itself as a break from the logic of pure marketisation, I illustrate the difficulties of escaping commercialisation at the policy level. This is not to say that APC-based gold OA is the only model for OA policymaking, but more that its impacts were so significant that they allowed publishers to reorient their business models entirely towards APCs and transformative agreements.

The Ideology of Plan S

In 2018, a coalition of eleven governmental and philanthropic research funders came together to develop Plan S, a bold statement intended to ensure immediate open access to all the research articles they fund. Concerned with the slow progress in OA uptake and the associated costs, this coalition ("cOAlition S") launched the policy claiming that it was "crucial to increase the impact of publications and the cost efficiency of the publication system"—speaking to their distaste not just for closed access, but for the commercial practices of the publishing industry, too.[10] Plan S is far-reaching in scale and disruptive in intent, requiring grant recipients to make their work immediately open access at the time of publication under the Creative Commons attribution licence (the most liberal of the Creative Commons licences). The policy states:

> With effect from 2021, all scholarly publications on the results from research funded by public or private grants provided by national, regional and international research councils and funding bodies, must be published in Open Access Journals, on Open Access Platforms, or made immediately available through Open Access Repositories without embargo.[11]

Based on ten principles (table 1 below), Plan S requires grantees to make their research freely available either through a journal (gold OA) or, if published in a subscription journal, through a repository (green OA). Crucially, Plan S will not support hybrid publishing (point 8), and so will not provide funding for authors to publish in journals that remain subscription-access while making individual articles freely accessible. Nonetheless, where a journal is fully OA—or transitioning to full OA—Plan S funders provide support for article-processing charges so that authors can publish in these journals.[12]

Although there is a great deal of underlying complexity within Plan S, and the details continually shift in response to reactions from the scholarly and publishing communities, an observable ideology of cOAlition S reflects faith in market principles to provide the desired outcome of OA publishing. In early 2022, the chief architect of Plan S, Robert-Jan Smits, coauthored a book detailing how the policy was created, shaped, and eventually put into practice. This somewhat hagiographic account of his role in the policy reveals the antagonism felt by cOAlition S towards the practices of commercial publishers, particularly larger presses such as Wiley, Elsevier, and Springer Nature. The antagonism was aimed towards industry concentration and high profit margins, or what the European Commission's open access envoy, Jean-Claude Burgelman, describes as "anyone making excessive money in a non-productive way. It's the monopoly position of their journals, with regards to controlling access to the service they provide, which is not acceptable."[13] To this extent, Plan S seeks a market realignment of the publishing industry and not a more radical intervention that prioritises, for example, nonprofit or university-led forms of publishing.

Initially, the architects of Plan S planned to intervene in the market by introducing a cap of €2,000 on the cost of article-processing charges to "stabilise the market and avoid an explosion in the price of APCs once OA became mandatory."[14] This

Table 1. The Plan S Principles

1. Authors or their institutions retain copyright to their publications. All publications must be published under an open licence, preferably the Creative Commons Attribution licence (CC BY), in order to fulfil the requirements defined by the Berlin Declaration;
2. The Funders will develop robust criteria and requirements for the services that high-quality Open Access journals, Open Access platforms, and Open Access repositories must provide;
3. In cases where high-quality Open Access journals or platforms do not yet exist, the Funders will, in a coordinated way, provide incentives to establish and support them when appropriate; support will also be provided for Open Access infrastructures where necessary;
4. Where applicable, Open Access publication fees are covered by the Funders or research institutions, not by individual researchers; it is acknowledged that all researchers should be able to publish their work Open Access;
5. The Funders support the diversity of business models for Open Access journals and platforms. When Open Access publication fees are applied, they must be commensurate with the publication services delivered and the structure of such fees must be transparent to inform the market and facilitate the potential standardisation and capping of payments of fees;
6. The Funders encourage governments, universities, research organisations, libraries, academies, and learned societies to align their strategies, policies, and practices, notably to ensure transparency.
7. The above principles shall apply to all types of scholarly publications, but it is understood that the timeline to achieve Open Access for monographs and book chapters will be longer and requires a separate and due process;
8. The Funders do not support the "hybrid" model of publishing. However, as a transitional pathway towards full Open Access

within a clearly defined time frame, and only as part of transformative arrangements, Funders may contribute to financially supporting such arrangements;

9. The Funders will monitor compliance and sanction noncompliant beneficiaries/grantees;
10. The Funders commit that when assessing research outputs during funding decisions they will value the intrinsic merit of the work and not consider the publication channel, its impact factor (or other journal metrics), or the publisher.

Source: Coalition S, "Plan S Principles," Plan S, accessed August 12, 2024, https://www.coalition-s.org/plan_s_principles/

proposal was eventually rejected by representatives of cOAlition S because of the "impracticality" of such an approach, according to Smits, although what the impracticality actually is remains unexplained.[15] Publishers themselves were furious about the possibility of caps on the price of APCs. The International Association of Scientific, Technical & Medical Publishers (STM) wrote, "Caps on APCs would restrict authors' choice of publication avenues for Gold Open Access, risk undermining quality and likely slow down the transition to a full Open Access environment."[16] Michael Clarke in the publishing-industry-backed blog *The Scholarly Kitchen* wrote that "the publishers that will thrive in such a market are those with economies of scale that publish a high volume of papers and, due to a broad editorial cascade, are able to publish a large percentage of the manuscripts they receive."[17] In response to publisher criticism, cOAlition S opted to require price transparency for the services provided by academic publishers instead of capped APCs. Through their "Journal Comparison Service," publishers voluntarily upload standardised information on the price they charge for the services they provide, such as editorial work, production, peer review, marketing/communication, and so on (listed as a percentage of the overall APC charged). This allows a comparison across the ecosystem of journals who decide to upload their data.

There are obvious drawbacks to the cOAlition S approach of price transparency, chief among them being the fact that it is not mandatory for publishers to upload their data to be eligible for publication fees from cOAlition S funders. Many publishers have uploaded their data, but many others have not, including the world's two biggest publishers, Elsevier and Springer.[18] The optional nature of price transparency significantly limits its strength as a form of regulation. Furthermore, even publishers who did upload their data give the percentages in terms of the ultimate price paid, not cost to the publisher, and so the end user of the data remains unaware of how much the publisher is investing in each article. Finally, individual researchers do not even have direct access to the data in question; because of commercial sensitivities, only libraries do. So even the original intention, that researchers will become price-sensitive in their publication practices, is unmet, simply because they will not have access to the data on which to base their decisions and compare publishers.

Although the Journal Comparison Service is only one aspect of Plan S, it is a significant component that reveals a great deal about the politics behind the policy and the limits of various market interventions in the academic publishing industry. The initially proposed price cap is an attempt to regulate extreme APC prices by placing a limit on them, a limit set at €2,000. Yet this was deemed unworkable by cOAlition S members. As Jean-Claude Burgelman explains, "Pricing is not a science issue, it's an economy issue. Of course the two are related and it has an effect, but as a science policymaker you have no instruments to determine prices."[19] For Burgelman, whose opinion ultimately prevailed, the role of the scientific policymaker is not to determine prices, but to require good scientific outcomes, in this case open access to research articles. Market forces will work their magic to keep prices in check, while not prohibiting scientists from publishing in more expensive venues if desired.

To be sure, an APC cap would not necessarily have desirable outcomes. For example, an APC of €2,000 is still incredibly expensive for unfunded researchers and those outside of wealthy universities and localities. For many researchers, the difference between €2,000 and €4,000 is irrelevant simply because they have no funding to cover APCs in the first place. Furthermore, limiting the price of an APC to €2,000 would be a significant market intervention precisely because it would force journals to cut costs while maintaining their profit margins. This austerity-seeking is common in debates around OA, leading to spurious articles about how much publishing *should* cost if you reduce it to an efficient, technological process, rather than one grounded in expertise and editorial care.[20] Many advocates of OA are committed to the idea that publishing should be cheap, failing to recognise that commercial publishing is already driven by the desire to make it an efficient, technological process to maximise profit. Nevertheless, we learn from the proposed APC cap just how difficult it is to intervene in the publishing market and how few tools policymakers have at their disposal to regulate the industry.

Turning to price "transparency," as with austerity, cOAlition S justifies their actions with respect to one of the key tenets of neoliberalism. For individuals to make informed decisions, the information on which they base their decisions must be "transparently" presented to them, rather than polluted by narrative or other forms of interpretation. For Garsten and Montoya, transparency is

> closely linked to a neoliberal ethos of governance that promotes individualism, entrepreneurship, voluntary forms of regulation and formalized types of accountability. It is powerful in that it is inscribed in political, financial and cultural documents, processes and policies that not only suggest, but push for, a certain normative order.[21]

Neoliberal approaches to transparency therefore appeal to notions of individual freedom and choice, particularly market-based choice, in a way that seeks to instantiate these as a "natural" form of governance. Clare Birchall argues that these neoliberal approaches to transparency promote a certain mode of disclosure that is "neutral, automated, systematic, efficient, lawful and regulatory," in opposition to the perceived "manipulated re-tellings" of narrative forms of disclosure.[22] This is a subjectivity represented, as Foucault describes, by the rational self-interested figure of *Homo oeconomicus*, the entrepreneur of the self, "being for himself his own capital, his own producer, the source of his earnings."[23] Under neoliberalism, *Homo oeconomicus* takes on an active, individualistic role as both producer and consumer of their own "satisfaction," compared with classical liberalism, in which *Homo oeconomicus* is a mere partner of exchange. This change of emphasis results in a governing rationality that promotes individual market participation that is well represented in the turn to transparency.

cOAlition S's desire for transparent data-sharing by publishers emerges from a commitment to neoliberal forms of governance. In advocating for transparency, especially in place of market-based interventions such as price caps, cOAlition S falls back on governance by market measurement, the idea that political decision-making should aim at creating ideal market conditions based primarily on deregulation and allowing the invisible hand of the market to create the best conditions. It is not that this form of governance is explicitly ideological in its application by policymakers; rather, it is seen as the natural way to create good policy—or else the ideology is so embedded in policymaking that it does not require further justification. This means that interventions like price caps or refusing to fund for-profit publications require much more robust justification because they are perceived as having a negative impact on the workings of a competitive market. This is why the publishing industry argued that price caps would penalise smaller publishers and lead to greater consolidation, irrespective of the fact that greater consolidation happened anyway without price caps, because consolidating is what markets do.

So, rather than working against the financialisation and consolidation of publishing, Plan S ends up reinforcing it through its commitment to the idea that academic publishing is best organised as a commercial industry. This situation is well summarised by Arianna Beccerill-Garcia of Redalyc:

> Attempts to deliver "transparent pricing" and "transformative agreements" are indicative of the way in which Plan S has been largely shaped by the interests of corporate pub-

> lishers and ultimately not those of the academic community, especially the academic community outside of the Global North. It's discouraging to admit that the main critique of Plan S is accurate: That it is a Eurocentric proposal that aims to remove paywalls to achieve open access, but which does not seek to reduce the earnings and concentration of power over academic publishing enjoyed by a small number of commercial publishers.[24]

I completely agree with this line of critique and I would like to go further and argue that Plan S also imposes a European/Northern understanding of subjectivity onto academic researchers, particularly the neoliberal individuation inherent in such an understanding of political decision-making. This individuation, as I now explore, works against the exploration and adoption of OA publishing as a common good.

The Individuation of Plan S

In 2018, cOAlition S launched a public consultation on its proposed policy. More than 600 responses were received from individuals and organisations, including libraries, universities, publishers, and learned societies from more than forty countries. The number of responses is illustrative of the depth of feeling around what Plan S was trying to achieve; many comments were critical of the proposed policy and its potential consequences for academic publishing. While I will not offer a full analysis of the responses here, the concerns presented by cOAlition S related to the impact of the policy on early-career researchers and learned societies, the value of full and immediate OA, and the pace and cost of the policy implementation.[25]

Despite these concerns, cOAlition S reiterated its commitment to the ten founding principles and to immediate OA, opting instead to soften its commitment to APC caps (cited above), to allow more restrictive licensing, to develop a route for funding some hybrid journals, and to delay the implementation process by one year.[26] In doing this, Plan S appeared to be more conciliatory in certain areas, but especially towards commercial publishers worried about the threat to their business. These fears were also presented as concern for the job progression of early-career researchers and about the fact that research assessment processes favour publications owned by larger commercial publishers. Due to the consultation process, the supposedly radical elements of the plan became less radical and more in service to the publishing market.

Yet the consultation itself was designed to introduce an element of accountability and public input from the "different communities and stakeholders" affected by Plan S.[27] It was designed to evoke a sense that the plan was in some ways a work of collective action or democracy, rather than the simple imposition of funder mandates onto these communities. Such consultation exercises are common in OA policymaking, intending to add to the legitimacy of the exercise. In practice, however, consultations are a way for policymakers to understand how to best make their directives *palatable* to the more powerful stakeholders in question. They are not, therefore, exercises in radical democracy in which all consultation responses are given equal weight.

cOAlition S operates a strategy of *interessement* in attempting to enroll other actors as allies and gain their support for the policy. Interessement is a key term in actor-network theory, introduced by Michael Callon to describe how an actor "attempts to impose and stabilize the identity of the other actors it defines through its problematization."[28] This occurs by one actor defining a problem or concept in a way that is recognisable and acceptable to all other actors in the network, particularly so that it aligns with their concerns, intentions, or goals. Callon describes this as a way of stabilising the network in order to "lock the allies into place." Interessement does not necessarily lead to a full alignment of the interests of all groups, but it does result in a pragmatic agreement on a particular issue.

cOAlition S employs interessement to obtain a tacit agreement on their policy and to "lock" the various stakeholders into place as allies. They do this with recourse to the consultation in order to understand what the stakeholders deem acceptable. The consultation provides a sense of legitimacy to the policy by granting a say to everyone affected by it, such as universities, publishers, researchers, and learned societies. Interessement therefore allows cOAlition S to take the "interests" of each actor into account and negotiate them into a policy. Yet the affected stakeholders have different degrees of power within the network, leading cOAlition S to prioritise certain viewpoints over others. For example, publishers, and particularly learned societies connected to commercial publishers, are in a strong position of influence over cOAlition S. If they argue that a funder intervention will harm their business, the policymakers are likely to listen. This is because of the coalition's commitment to a neoliberal ideology, which judges the efficacy of policymaking by the extent to which it conforms to market logic.

The conservative voices of learned societies were also of use to the coalition's strategy. Many learned societies receive most of their funding from publishers, through the sale of subscriptions to society journals, and so the views of publishers and learned societies are frequently in alignment on OA. However, learned societies also represent the voices of the academics who govern the society, particularly early-career researchers who societies often claim need protection from OA publishing.[29] cOAlition S was able to use the consultation responses from learned societies as representative of academic voices more generally, despite the societies' having a financial interest in a conservative approach to OA that protects the revenue of commercial publishers. The positioning of different actors indicates how the interests of some stakeholders are valued more highly than those of others. This imbalance of power is clearly noticeable in the policy's approach to hybrid forms of OA, which were originally intended to be entirely excluded from cOAlition S funding, but were slowly rehabilitated through interventions, including "transformative" journals that must commit to converting to OA by a certain period of time. Though such journals are still hybrid publications, cOAlition S was willing to fund publication in those that made this commitment; there was no penalty for journals that did not transition to OA within the specified time frame except their no longer being considered "transformative."

Another theme in the response to Plan S was how the policy on hybrid journals may inhibit individual academic freedom.[30] This led cOAlition S to devise an approach to allow authors to publish in hybrid journals using the so-called rights-retention "strategy." This legalistic strategy requires authors to signal to the publisher their intent to deposit their article in a repository, enabling compliance with Plan S without paying an article-processing charge. They do so by including the following terminology in the article's financial disclosure:

> This research was funded in whole or in part by [funder and grant number]. For the purpose of Open Access, the author has applied a CC BY public copyright licence to any Author Accepted Manuscript (AAM) version arising from this submission.[31]

By agreeing to publish articles that include this phrase, publishers accept the conditions outlined by authors. This "prior notification" takes precedence over any subsequent transfer of copyright to the publisher, meaning that authors retain the rights to share their final, editorially accepted manuscript in accordance with the licence they choose.

It is tempting to view the rights-retention strategy as a simple and convenient way for researchers to comply with the OA policy without paying an article-processing charge. While this assessment is true to an extent, it fails to consider the fact that researchers are being put in a difficult position between funders and publishers. In particular, publishers are under no obligation to accept articles using the rights-retention strategy, and many are lining up to reject or reroute papers that contain the declaration above.[32] Bearing in mind that this strategy was designed to allow early-career researchers to submit to the journal of their choice, it seems clear that more precarious researchers are shouldering the individual responsibility for compliance with the policy, whereas cOAlition S is collectively willing to support commercial publishers through their transitional journal route.

When viewed through the lens of interessement, we can see that commercial logic dictates the power structure around which cOAlition S is basing its decisions. Individual researchers are forced to lock horns with publishers to make their accepted manuscripts available in a repository, while the bigger publishers are gifted new, lucrative routes to compliance in the form of transformative journals. Interessement in a neoliberal policy environment cannot help but reduce everything to economic interests, meaning that powerful economic actors benefit and researchers are responsible for navigating the new world of OA publishing. This is also why cOAlition S promotes transparency and individual market-based decision-making.

To take this further, Plan S can be theorised in accordance with what Annemarie Mol terms a "logic of choice," which justifies an action or intervention by the extent to which it promotes individual choice through market participation. Looking specifically at healthcare, Mol interrogates how diabetes is treated in various ways along a continuum between *choice* and *care*. The former prioritises individual decision-making and draws a "limit" on what treatment is offered, while the latter promotes a form of treatment that is "open-ended" and based on a continual process of supporting the patient in their unique circumstances.[33] Although both "care" and "choice" can refer to market participation, the discourse of "customer choice" is intimately connected with the increased marketisation of healthcare. Plan S is based on a similar logic of choice that seeks to create ideal conditions for individuals to interact autonomously with the publishing market.

Through a strategy of interessement based on this logic of choice, cOAlition S relies on and reinforces a subjectivity grounded in liberal individualism and the rational, self-interested person represented by Foucault's *Homo oeconomicus*. These actors are grouped into different collections of individuals who share the same interests, and the policymakers then order these interests according to varying degrees of power. All of this is based on the idea that policymaking is about creating the right conditions for individuals to make good, self-interested (economic) choices. As Mol shows, this choice-based logic assumes that:

> We start out as separate individuals and that we begin to form a collective as we are added together. This means that it frames individuals as building blocks that jointly make a larger whole. The building blocks are named in different ways. In the market variant of the logic of choice they are called "customers."[34]

By dividing actors in this way, cOAlition S continues to position academic publishing as an external service to higher education, as a product to a consumer, instead of attempting to unpick its more pernicious features resulting from commercialisation.

Indeed, the idea of publishers as mere "service providers" is a common theme in the rhetoric of cOAlition S and its supporters.[35] It is deployed to emphasise the choice that researchers have between different providers: if they do not like the conditions of one service provider, they can simply take their business elsewhere. This is because publishers are "substitutable" and can "compete and innovate according to conditions set by the scholarly community," rather than being embedded within this community and a necessary part of it.[36] This perfect market of easily replaceable service providers is the desired end goal of Plan S—and neoliberal logic more generally—and therefore represents no challenge to the marketisation of publishing. So, despite positioning itself in opposition to the market excesses of commercial actors, and initially declaring its intention to boldly intervene in the publishing market through regulation, Plan S simply rehearses all the conditions of marketisation to which ethical forms of OA publishing were responding in the first instance. But how, then, does Plan S relate to ideas of the commons?

The Commons Without Care/Care Without the Commons

In an article entitled "From Coalition to Commons: Plan S and the Future of Scholarly Communication," Rob Johnson explores the work of cOAlition S from the perspective of Elinor Ostrom's ideas relating to polycentricity and adaptive governance, which illustrate how governance should be a process—not a fixed plan—and should ideally be devolved to as many decision-making centres as practical (polycentric).[37] For Johnson, Plan S is an exercise in multi-stakeholder cooperation and "collective action by funders" to bring about a harmonious and influential policy. I show above, for example, how cOAlition S members exercised democratic self-governance to vote on proposals such as whether to cap article-processing charges. The members are not all necessarily in full alignment, but they still work out the best way to proceed with the policy. Johnson writes that three assumptions underpin the development of Plan S:

- The research literature should be treated as an intellectual commons.
- Collective action by funders can be effective in creating such a commons.
- Scholarly publishing services should be delivered, at least in part, by a "regulated market."[38]

Johnson rightly notes that certain understandings of the commons are not incompatible with neoliberal economics. Indeed, we see here that treating the commons as a mere resource will lead to exactly the kinds of market-centric approaches to policymaking that I identify above. The coalition is happy to be guided by the idea that it is desirable to consider publishing to be an external commercial service to higher education, and not something that would benefit from being positioned within and led by academic communities.

As I theorised in the previous chapter, a more politically progressive approach to the commons is one conceived as a mode of production based on the self-organisation of labour, not just the free sharing of resources. The resource being created and maintained, in this case academic publications, is of course important, but just as important are the manner of its creation and the communities that use and maintain it. Plan S for the most part fails to engage with the communities that currently use and maintain the publishing ecosystem, and instead positions them as blocs of individuals to be ordered by their interests (through "interessement") and successfully managed as part of the policy environment. This is the problem with top-down policies that require open access as the endpoint without adequately engaging with the underlying ways these resources are produced. This illustrates how, restating Johnson above, Plan S considers their idea of the scholarly commons to be achievable through market regulation rather than any deeper or radical intervention.

What is missing from this conception of the commons is the relational, local, and community-based understanding of OA that is found in initiatives at the margins, including some of those explored in the next chapter. These community-specific features are absent from the "intellectual commons" as conceived by cOAlition S, primarily because it does not take into account the relational, open-ended *care-based* understandings of publishing. Publishing, for cOAlition S, is always already a commercial operation, and so attention need not be paid to these things. Instead, returning to Annemarie Mol, Plan S is organised according to a commercial logic of choice that treats researchers (and libraries) as customers, when it should be prioritising a logic of care that attends to the position of publishing within scholarly communities. Mol writes, "Care is not a transaction in which something is exchanged (a product against a price); but an interaction in which the action goes back and forth (in an ongoing process)."[39] It is this processual understanding that is elided by marketised forms of publishing; under commercial OA, publishing becomes a pure choice-based transaction by individuals operating in the market.

I am arguing here that publishing needs to be understood as both entirely embedded within particular communities and as emanating from community interactions: it is a process of care, which is why it is well suited to a conception of the commons as the self-organisation of labour. For example, a journal is a form of sociality that brings a community of people together and leads to the creation and dissemination of knowledge. It cannot be reduced to a market transaction or service, and instead requires treatment as a community process—not just the community of academics reading, writing, and reviewing the papers, but the various forms of labour that go into publishing, including editing, production, copyediting, design, preservation, and so on. When publishing a journal is considered just a commercial service, as Plan S does, it tends to devalue this labour, which is increasingly outsourced to unpaid academics or to underpaid workers in the Global South, or it is automated and funnelled through cookie-cutter production processes. This is the logic of choice at work: researchers pay an APC and in return get a certain kind of product.

It would not be correct to say that Plan S is responsible for the "care-less" approach to publishing they are promoting; it is simply the business of publishing to reduce costs where possible. But in accepting this business approach, Plan S reinforces it further, reducing the possibility of using OA publishing for radical purposes or to undermine the commercial imperative. In many ways, the tendency to treat publishing as a transaction is embedded in the culture of higher education and encouraged by universities, who judge the quality of a piece of research by where it's published, including through assessment exercises such as the UK's Research Excellence Framework. For many researchers, particularly those on precarious contracts, publishing *is* to some extent transactional in that an article in a high-impact journal or a book with a prestigious press will improve their chances of job promotion and career progression, especially in light of the academic job market and the general defunding of public education.[40] Considering publishing in this transactional way is also a way to devalue, or at least underappreciate, the processual and careful nature of research communication. Indeed, the argument often follows that the publishing process itself is unnecessary, or almost *pernicious*, due to the profit margins of commercial publishers, leading many to conclude that we no longer need to support the labour of publishing and can instead "completely ditch academic journals and decentralise everything."[41]

Devaluing the labour of publishing is actually a form of conservatism, not least because this labour is often performed by underpaid editorial and production colleagues. Furthermore, such arguments from austerity represent a failure of the imagination around what publishing is and could be. A race to the bottom in terms of costs means that publishing is only justified as a minimum service requirement, not a rich practice of community-led knowledge production that needs to be supported, financially and otherwise. This austerity-driven lack of imagination is noticeable in the large-scale funder platforms for OA that many of cOAlition S members are now hosting. Open Research Europe, for example, is a publishing platform for researchers funded by the Horizon 2020 scheme.[42] Managed by the for-profit publisher F1000, owned by Taylor & Francis, the platform illustrates the removal of human expertise from publishing, replacing it with an automated cookie-cutter platform with little editorial oversight. Automated funder platforms are the logical conclusion of Plan S and its appreciation of publishing as mere service. cOAlition S seeks only to make research articles open access; it is neither able to undo nor particularly interested in undoing the impacts of commerciality. This is the commons without care: freely accessible open access articles with no thought about the processes, communities, localities, and labours that make up the bibliodiversity of publishing and research communication more broadly.[43] This global approach to the commons is indiscriminate and homogenising, echoing Maria Mies's argument that there is "no commons without community," because the commons is necessarily a local, community-centric activity.[44]

Yet perhaps paradoxically, Plan S does rely on a huge amount of relational and affective labour in academic libraries. This care work is a common feature of OA policies, requiring library staff to assume the burden of policy compliance in an open-ended nontransactional manner. When a funder introduces a new policy or change, libraries must quickly adapt, generate guidance, and then disseminate the new rules so that academics are aware of their obligations. The additional care work can be seen, following Star and Strauss, as a form of invisible work: labour that is taken for granted and "relegated to a background of expectation."[45] Librarians are forced to assume more responsibility for the additional burden of training and assistance, alongside their other tasks. Because this labour is open-ended and relational, administrators can relegate it to the class of work that is not "legitimate, individuated and traceable across settings."[46] The labour of care is made invisible when it is not valued in an institutional environment.

Librarianship is frequently positioned as a feminised profession, despite the disproportionate presence of men in leadership roles.[47] Such professions, as Kim England argues, are more likely to involve work grounded in care and "labours of love" than those based in waged work. She writes:

> This gendering of work has its ideological and historical roots in the social and spatial separation of waged work from social reproduction. "Work" became constituted as "economically productive" waged-labour that took place outside the home. Housekeeping, caring for family members and other "domestic" activities became non-marketized "labours of love" primarily associated within the private sphere of family and home, and assumed to be primarily the responsibility of wives and mothers. The construction

> of a socio-spatial boundary separating "work"-production-public from care-reproduction-private devalues and obscures activities defined as "women's work."[48]

In a similar vein, Roxanne Shirazi describes some of the features that define librarianship, such as emotional and reproductive labour, and how librarians are positioned as operating in the service of scholars rather than alongside them as equals. Shirazi characterises this as work that "reproduces the academy" but is "reduced to (and devalued as) 'service.'"[49]

Plan S reflects this understanding of librarianship as feminised and service-based care work that performs the function of policy-based compliance, not as an equal partner valued for its scholarly contribution, but more as a human infrastructure for support. In many ways, the labour of library workers reflects care *without* the commons; rather, library workers become infrastructural objects for supporting the policy environment. This approach to library labour reflects Silvia Federici's argument about how under capitalism, "women themselves became the commons, as their work was defined as a natural resource, laying outside the sphere of market relations."[50] OA policymakers look to libraries to sort out the fine detail of OA compliance, often on top of their pre-existing roles as information specialists. All of this work sits outside of market relations, and is devalued as a result.

"Sneak into the University"

Although I have shown that Plan S mostly shores up the regressive commercial-based publishing environment, it is worth considering whether it, and the OA policy environment more generally, opens space for more radical and ethical approaches to publishing that do not simply recapitulate all the values of marketisation. Which is to say, are there any benefits to the policy-led shift from closed to open access for the forms of publishing that operate outside or against the market, or does it only work against the possibility of such a radical open-access commons?

To answer this question, which is above all a political question, it is worth looking to Stefano Harney and Fred Moten's notion of the undercommons, a shared fugitive space carved out of the university that refuses its neoliberal sensibilities while allowing radical forms of thought and sociality to exist. They write:

> [I]t cannot be denied that the university is a place of refuge, and it cannot be accepted that the university is a place of enlightenment. In the face of these conditions one can only sneak into the university and steal what one can. To abuse its hospitality, to spite its mission, to join its refugee colony, its gypsy encampment, to be in but not of—this is the path of the subversive intellectual in the modern university.[51]

To "steal" from the university is, for Harney and Moten, one way to navigate its capitalist logic. The university gathers resources that can be utilised for emancipatory ends, provided one can devise strategic ways to access them. This means accepting the liberal, individualistic, enlightenment nature of the university, which cannot be displaced, but can be taken advantage of.

I would like to suggest that the turn to OA facilitated by the governmental and philanthropic funder landscape affords the opportunity for radical presses to access resources that would not have been made available had this turn not happened. Funding for OA exists, and projects of all different ideological leanings can access it. This is in part due to the fluid nature of "open access" as a concept, a boundary object as I theorise elsewhere, that means many things to many groups, but is recognisable enough to maintain its identity as a concept.[52] To this extent, many of us are attempting to squat within the OA movement to nurture the commons (as outlined in the next two chapters). This is one of the main reasons I am interested in OA: it provides the resources for a counter-hegemonic project against market-led forms of publishing. Although this project may stay at the margins, it is real and exists within, across, and outside the various movements for OA.

Indeed, we are now seeing disquiet in policymaker circles around the ways these policies have led to commercial capture. For example, the Council of European Member States has recently agreed on a memo that specifically calls for nonprofit models and a move away from author fees in promotion of the "diamond" mode of OA, which does not exclude either or authors or readers on economic grounds.[53] This is a bold perspective and shows a new direction of travel for the EU, one that could possibly result in freeing up funding for community-led publishing initiatives. However, as with Plan S, what started out as a bold plan to intervene in the publishing market was watered down in favour of the political status quo. There is conceptual flexibility to terms like "author fees" and "nonprofit," and the devil is in the implementation details. For example, many publishing agreements between universities and publishers do not rely on author fees but instead on prepayment by universities and no further financial transaction involving the author. Similarly, do publishing platforms (like Open Research Europe, discussed above) count as nonprofit if the underlying technology is provided by a for-profit organisation?

Furthermore, even if diamond OA does become the next frontier for publishing, there are two distinct ideologies from which it could emerge. The first relates to the publishing ecosystem of small journals and presses led by scholars, libraries, and other nonprofit and community-led initiatives. The second reflects the rehabilitation of commercial publishers as service providers based on a "techno-solutionism" that assumes humans are mostly surplus to requirements in publishing or that academics and low-paid outsourced labour can just do it all. The former, which I am arguing for in this book, requires financial support, and the view that publishing has scholarly value that is currently diminished by the publishing market. The latter is based on austerity—it takes as its *primary aim* that there is money to be saved in the turn to OA.

Ultimately, Plan S will be shaped by these two competing publishing futures, and cOAlition S will have to make a decision based on their merits and drawbacks. The two approaches are not mutually exclusive and may resonate differently in different publishing contexts, yet they do reflect alternate politics and visions of a publishing future. cOAlition S deploys rhetoric that is critical of commercial publishing while continuing to reinforce commercial modes of production; it remains to be seen whether they will respond to the burgeoning diamond future of OA publishing, or if they will simply ignore it and double down on the policy framework that most benefits the consolidated publishing industry.

The next chapter explores an ecosystem of scholar-led publishers representing an alternative conception of what open access could be. Through this exploration, we start to see where the OA publishing commons might exist and how it offers a counterpoint to the marketised forms of OA depicted within this chapter.

Chapter 3

Radical Experiments in Scholar-Led Publishing

Moving away from the regressive output-focused visions of Plan S and associated OA policies, I now turn my attention to projects at the margins of publishing that offer a counterpoint to the marketisation of both subscription and OA publishing. The presses discussed here are entirely managed by scholars—either within or outside the confines of the traditional university—and represent a distinct model of OA publishing that offers promise for a critical and progressive future of scholarly communication. By analysing the discourse and practice of these presses, I attempt to reveal their thinking and doings, including the variety of ways in which this ecosystem of small presses might be nurtured to form a response to dominant models of commercial publishing (as chapter 4 discusses). I am guided by the question of what scholar-led publishing teaches us about the commons and how it relates to the broader movements agitating for OA publishing. The work discussed here is a mixture of the history of scholar-led publishing and interviews with scholar-led publishers, theorised in accordance with work on care and the commons.

While the presses discussed here are by no means the only site of ethical publishing activity within OA, they do represent a coherent bloc that operates outside the dominant commercial publishing hegemony. The decision of academics to publish their own journals and books has in part been enabled by digital technologies that allow self-sufficiency outside of professional forms of publishing. However, this kind of publishing is not new, and is in many ways a continuation of various forms of scholar control that have always been a part of publishing. I hope to show how, through strategic alliances with other publishing initiatives, scholar-led publishing reflects an opportunity to work through the marketisation of OA brought on by the commercial publishing industry.

What Is Scholar-Led Publishing?

Academic publishing is clearly oriented around scholars and scholarship. Journals are edited by academic editors and reviewers, who marshal the work of academic authors through a publishing process that is ultimately aimed at an academic readership. To this extent, publishing is and always has been "led" by scholars who provide the labour and content for publishing and add legitimacy to it through the peer-review process. However, there has also been a long-held tension between business concerns and editorial independence, not just since the marketisation of publishing, but historically too. For example, Dawson and Topham illustrate how societies in the early nineteenth century were continually grappling with the need to appeal to their members and the financial imperative to appeal to a broader audience of the interested public.[1] Yet the difference between then and now is that then, learned societies themselves controlled all aspects of the publishing operation, both editorially and financially, while today the business side is predominantly outsourced to commercial industry and driven by the needs of these businesses. Learned societies are unable to escape the trappings of revenue generation even if they are not profit-focused.

In 1963, as Aileen Fyfe and colleagues show, the Royal Society produced a "code for the publication of new scientific journals," largely in response to the flurry of journals being created on the commercial market and concerns about the loss of editorial independence in the drive for revenue. Within the code, the Royal Society members wrote that the "ideal body to run a journal is a scientific society, but if that is not possible, then editorial and financial policy should be in the hands of academics, and that copyright should be retained by authors."[2] This attempt to codify the future relationship between society and publisher suggests that societies were worried about losing control of publishing in a commercial world. Their fears were well founded, as much of this book has explored so far, and scholar governance of the publishing industry was increasingly reduced in the years that followed.[3]

The reduction in scholar governance and oversight is one of the common reasons cited by editorial boards for leaving their publisher and starting a new journal elsewhere. This trend has hastened in recent years as editors push back on the commercial practices of the publishing industry.[4] For example, the editors of the Elsevier journal *NeuroImage* resigned due to the "greed" of its publisher and its refusal to reduce article processing charges to what the editors considered an affordable level.[5] Similarly, the editors of *Critical Public Health*, a Taylor & Francis journal, resigned in protest at "the limited role the publisher sees for the editorial team and board."[6] Part of this decision was based on the publisher's move to an OA model that prioritises article fees and increased journal volume that the editors claimed "significantly eroded our ability to set strategic direction."[7] In each case, the editors went on to form an entirely new journal in partnership with an institutional publisher. Academic governance is a key site of struggle over the marketised publishing industry.

But what about those publishing projects that are *entirely managed* by academics with little recourse to publishers or other third parties? This is the notion of scholar-led publishing that I explore in this chapter. A model growing in popularity, scholar-led publishing collectives organise and maintain the entire publishing process. Scholar-led publishing represents a distinct model that has always been a feature of the transition to OA, even if a somewhat peripheral one. Today, scholar-led publishers are frequently positioned as emblematic of the diamond OA model that does not charge for either access or publication. They are part of a flourishing ecosystem alongside other institutionally led publishing projects, such as library publishers and open access university presses. While there is overlap between these scholar/library/university publishing assemblages, I foreground those organised by scholars.

"Scholars" itself is a vague term, and I do not want to suggest any particular elitism in the view that scholars may be better positioned than others to publish their own books and journals. The fact is that many disciplinary experts—those contributing scholarly research to their own field—already manage publishing projects. They range from graduate students to senior and retired academics; they could be based within a university or outside it, and usually see their publishing projects as an extension of their scholarly work (as I shall show). I want to suggest that this connection between disciplinary expertise and the practice of publishing is what makes scholar-led publishing a unique and worthwhile model to explore. It entails a kind of care that is absent from much commercial publishing, a care that could be re-instantiated in academic publishing through OA forms of scholar-led publishing.

The descriptor "scholar-led" is important not because it connotes a specific ethics or set of values, but because it separates the term from a more general or normative understanding of terms such as "community-led" that evoke a nonspecific grassroots quality that usually remains undefined. The term "community," as Raymond Williams writes, "seems never to be used unfavourably, and never to be given any positive opposing or distinguishing term."[8] It is a useful rhetorical device, and indeed "scholar-led" does connote the benefits of being in a "big tent" of community-led projects (as Tobias Steiner writes), but is less useful as an analytical term that specifies the actors that constitute this community and what they do.[9] For Melanie Schlosser and Catherine Mitchell of the Library Publishing Coalition, this ambiguity leaves us with "practical questions about what defines community membership, how governance is structured, what the funding model looks like, and who supplies the publishing infrastructure."[10] Similarly, for Steiner, it is important to differentiate between scholar-led and other approaches to publishing because doing so "helps to avoid glossing over the manifold organisational, legal, financial, and/or conceptual differences that exist between the various actors in the larger publishing ecosystem, and the corresponding politics that each group of actors bring to the table."[11] Scholar-led publishing therefore sits within a complex web of community-led publishing projects that reflect a multitude of politics and practices. It is also, as Marcel Wrzesinski argues, a practice that is "not properly acknowledged by the academic reputation system or the publishing industry," meaning that scholar-led publishing is rarely undertaken for material or financial gain.[12]

Scholar-Led Publishing and the Early Web

Early documents concerning the birth of the web show that public research dissemination was a key motivation for Tim Berners-Lee and colleagues, who wrote in 1991 that "the project started with the philosophy that much academic information should be freely available to anyone. It aims to allow information sharing within internationally dispersed teams, and the dissemination of information by support groups."[13] Emerging from an academic environment rather than private industry meant that the technologies were not geared towards commercial gain, and users were given a high degree of freedom that allowed a host of niche and experimental academic projects to flourish—or what early OA advocate Stevan Harnad described as the "esoteric" literature that was not primarily aimed at financial gain for its authors but had intrinsic academic worth.[14]

Scholar-led OA was a notable feature of publishing on the early web. Journals such as *Surfaces*, the *Bryn Mawr Classical Review*, *Psycoloquy*, *Postmodern Culture*, and *Public-Access Computer Systems Review* were entirely managed by academics utilising FTP and listserv software and subsequently the web and now-defunct Gopher protocol. In practice, these journals did not consider limiting access to online research simply because few people had access to the web and those who did were usually based at universities, a point also made by Paul Ginsparg about the early days of the arXiv preprint server.[15] But public access was not just a natural or inertial feature of this research landscape. Many early scholar-led journals were clear that public access to their scholarship was of great importance and a goal for the future of publishing. For example, in 1990, the editor of the *Public-Access Computer Systems Review*, Charles W. Bailey Jr., hypothesised:

> As computer network interconnections and capabilities increase, the "global village" may become a much more immediate day-to-day reality in libraries. Government-funded networks for businesses and general citizens may also develop over time, and these networks may be linked to scholarly networks. Both of these potential developments could greatly increase the size and heterogeneity of the network user population.[16]

Even before the web was invented, and long before internet access was common for the general public, early scholar-led journals could see the potential of networked technologies, not just for distributing scholarship but for increasing its audience as well. These journals were developed without access controls, and the hope was that the audience of scholarly material would increase as internet access did. This point is emphasised by one of the *Bryn Mawr Classical Review* founders, James J. O'Donnell, who, writing five years after the journal's launch in 1990, claimed that the network has increased the diversity of their audience, specifically to include "people who do not define themselves as professional classicists" and what they term the "Enlightened General Reader."[17] For O'Donnell, classical scholarship ran the risk of becoming a "hermetic club for experts, dwindling over the years, if we do not find ways to address a wider public with our best work."[18] The journal was seen as one way to reach this wider public.

This desire for public access to research was also noticeable in the work of *Postmodern Culture*, whose editors wrote in 1990 that "for a publication in electronic media to succeed in serving even the most traditional purposes, such publication obviously needs to be available to the public—to students, to researchers, and to interested readers."[19] This commitment to broad access was grounded further in a subsequent article written in 1996 by *Postmodern Culture* cofounder Eyal Amiran, who argued that the electronic serial fulfils the "utopian promise of the serial form" because it heralds a new era of "equality of information and access."[20] Public access to research was clearly a unifying theme across the early-scholar-led journals.

While many of the early scholar-led presses were based in the sciences, especially tech-savvy disciplines such as mathematics and computer science (as Hitchcock et al.'s 1996 survey of STEM online journals reveals[21]), it is important to emphasise that the humanities and social sciences were present, too. For example, *Surfaces* and *Postmodern Culture* were key journals of critical theory research, while the *Bryn Mawr Classical Review* became an important publication in classical studies. The presence of scholar-led journals publishing interpretative and qualitative research, particularly within critical theory, goes against the idea that OA publishing was founded by the sciences and thrust onto unwilling humanities and social sciences. Instead, one needs a more expansive understanding of the genealogies of OA that reveal the early presence of critical theorists and scholar-activists. One could even, as Rebekka Kiesewetter does, identify part of the genealogy of OA in the activism of "feminist, queer, anti-colonial, anti-racist, and labour movements active since the 1980s."[22] Scholar- and activist-led collectives such as Kitchen Table Press, Midnight Notes, and Precarias each organised their publications self-sufficiently and as a praxis of activism. For Kiesewetter, scholar-led presses represent an entanglement of this activist publishing with the technological self-sufficiency that in part led to the OA movement.

As early as the mid-1990s, this newfound technological self-sufficiency was predicted to cause the downfall of traditional publishers, and especially scholarly journals. In an article from 1995, "The Tragic Loss or Good Riddance? The Impending Demise of Traditional Scholarly Journals," Andrew M. Odlyzko wrote:

> What would be the role of publishers in the projected system? Scholars can run electronic journals themselves, with no financial subsidies or subscription fees, using only the spare capacity of the computers and networks that are provided to them as part of their job. [. . .] There is more work for authors and editors in such a system than with traditional print journals, but advances in technology are decreasing the effort that is required.[23]

As the web grew in popularity, an increasing number of scholar collectives embraced the opportunity to create and manage their own journals. They did so not as a commercial endeavour—

often relying on little to no financial support as Odlyzko predicted—but as something facilitated by the absence of commercial pressures in the digital age and by the freedom this offered. For Stevan Harnad, this new approach to research dissemination would strongly influence the publishing industry by making it mostly redundant, forcing publishers to become mere providers of peer review and "optional add-ons."[24]

In many ways, as I have argued elsewhere, these early presses reflect what Christopher Kelty terms "recursive publics," those self-sufficient collectives concerned with the "material and practical maintenance and modification of the technical, legal, practical, and conceptual means of [their] own existence as a public."[25] For Kelty, focusing on the free-software movement, these technologically enabled collectives represent a challenge to power through their production of "actually existing alternatives." They are not merely agitating for change, but creating, maintaining, and reproducing it, too, through their work of coding, sharing, and self-reliance. Similarly, as I hope to now show, scholar-led publishers are recursive publics in how they are producing these actually existing alternatives to the commercial publishing industry. But what are they publishing, how are they doing it, and what motivates them? What does this tell us about the practical possibilities of the OA publishing commons I have been theorising so far?

Scholar-Led Publishing Today: Resistance, Critique, and Experimentation

To explore the motivations and practices of a number of scholar-led publishers, I now present secondary data analysis of interviews conducted for the report "Changing Publishing Ecologies.

A Landscape Study of New University Presses and Academic-led Publishing."[26] The interview data is openly available on the Jisc repository and provides a rich account of the rationale and practices of scholar-led publishers.[27] The report was commissioned to understand the characteristics of new university-press and scholar-led initiatives, concluding with a series of recommendations to "help support and foster new developments."[28] This chapter will focus on twelve scholar-led presses, all in the humanities and social sciences: MayFly Books, Roving Eye Press/Electric Press, punctum books, Mattering Press, Media Commons Press, Meson Press, Open Humanities Press, Open Book Publishers, Goldsmiths Press, Language Science Press, and Counter Press.

It is clear from the interviews that academics set up their own OA presses for a variety of reasons. The publishing industry was simply not meeting the needs of many scholar-led presses, or publishing the kinds of content they wanted to see. For example, the German publisher Meson Press was founded to offer an English-language press to nonnative English speakers, for whom "it is not always very easy to get into existing academic presses."[29] Nor, co-founder Mercedes Bunz notes, was there a press in Europe specifically dedicated to media studies, and so Meson was founded to meet this need. Similarly, Craig Saper launched Roving Eye Press to "rediscover" and publish the out-of-print works of Bob Brown, while MediaCommons Press sought to experiment with forms of scholarship that were not "strictly textual, or print-based, or linear in format."[30] Such divergent motivations reveal the presses' desire to meet a disciplinary or cultural need not currently met by the publishing industry.

However, it is also apparent that many of the presses launched without an explicit understanding of what they were going to publish and how. There is a sense of informality, playfulness, or happenstance surrounding some of the publishing efforts analysed here. For Stephen Connelly of Counter Press, book publishing was the simple formalisation of successful online blogposts that the editors felt would benefit from being collected together.[31] Similarly, Mattering Press had enjoyed organising workshops together as a collective, and "happened on" the idea of publishing books as a next project, while Chris Land of *Ephemera* and MayFly Books describes the "arrogance of young PHD students thinking that they knew better than anybody else."[32] *Ephemera* and Mayfly in particular represent a fleeting or transient approach to publishing (as represented by their names) that eschews formality or explicitly thought-through publishing programmes.

We might conceive of these divergent motivations as a "labour of love," following Andrea E. Pia et al., who position scholar-led publishing as "unremunerated, off-work time that is freely given as a result of political, emotional and otherwise idealistic investment in projects that transcend the quest for academic prestige and seek to transform the publishing system from within."[33] Scholar-led publishing stands outside the marketised publishing industry in both ideological and material senses. It often entails scholars withdrawing and redirecting their labour towards their own editorial labours of love, thus creating the material conditions for their own publishing projects to flourish.

Even though many of the presses launched with the intention of representing something different than the publishing industry offers, the strongest theme to emerge from the interviews was how each press adopts a stance of critique and resistance towards various aspects of the politics of knowledge production. This critique reflects a desire to reclaim control of publishing, particularly from large commercial publishers, in favour of publishing programmes focused on a variety of ethical, political, and disciplinary interventions in academic publishing. Grassroots, scholar-led approaches to OA differ in their values from both the commercial OA landscape and the top-down policies examined in the previous chapter. It is important to not consider the values on display as held by all the presses or as part of a coherent philosophy regarding alternative forms of OA publishing. Instead, such alternatives should be seen as providing a space for different values and practices that traditional publishing may not permit. This idea of bibliodiversity is explored more fully in the next chapter.

Many of the interviewed presses also exist in opposition to the profit-making activities of commercial publishing. This is a key theme of the OA movement, and all the presses analysed here operate on a nonprofit basis. Sebastian Nordhoff at Lang Sci Press describes the high prices charged by commercial publishers for books that prohibit their sharing, leading him to conclude, "The interests of profit-oriented publishers are incompatible with those of the researchers."[34] Chris Land of Counter Press explained the press's motivation of "trying to take academic publishing back into academic control, resisting the commercialisation, the firewalls, all those kinds of things."[35] Similarly, Rupert Gatti of Open Book Publishers describes the frustrations felt by one of the press's cofounders, whose monograph on Russian literature was too expensive for people living in Russia to purchase. Consequently, she sends copies of the book to Russian libraries at her own expense.[36] The presses therefore operate in opposition to commercial publishing and see OA as one way to resist profit-making in scholarly research.

Connected with this critique of commercialisation is the idea that academic-led presses are willing to adopt the kinds of practices that traditional publishers refuse for commercial reasons. Many of the presses therefore experiment in form, subject matter, content, and notions of authorship in ways that traditional presses do not permit because they are not monetizable. Eileen Joy, for example, characterises "traditional" publisher approaches to monograph publishing as "Sell this overpriced book to roughly 250, 300 libraries, recoup the money and the profit, and then shut the book down. Drop it off the list, let it go out of print. Who cares? We got our money back and then we move on to the next book: they are all about high volume, low quality."[37] For some of those interviewed, traditional publishing carries with it the need to recuperate costs at the expense of quality, diversity, and experimentation.

Similarly, Kathleen Fitzpatrick describes how MediaCommons Press was formed in order to disseminate open, born-digital, annotatable works that publishers were too risk-averse or ill-equipped to publish themselves:

> The main goal, really, was to be able to facilitate that kind of conversation around the material that we wanted to have. This was in 2009, when we released Planned Obsolescence. It was a very easy process for us, as individuals, to be able to set up a server running WordPress, to be able to create the template, use the plug-ins that we need, set it up under the auspices of MediaCommons, and draw together an audience

> that would have the discussion that we were looking to have. A press at that time was really not able, in the same way, to support that kind of work. They weren't technologically equipped. They didn't have the skill bases that they needed in order to do that. They had a necessary risk averseness, simply because of the ways that their budgets functioned, that wouldn't allow them to do that kind of experimentation without a whole lot of study, a whole lot of preparation, and a whole lot of practical concerns that, as an individual, I simply didn't have at that time.[38]

There is a theme here: that the traditional publishing industry is conservative by its very nature. It is reflective of restrictive business models that encourage standardisation, limited budgetary allocations, or simply a lack of expertise in the technology needed for such experimentation. In contrast, scholar-led publishers can determine not just what they publish but *how* they publish. For Fitzpatrick, setting up MediaCommons herself was easier and more practical than working with a pre-existing press. Scholar-led publishing offers a kind of freedom and flexibility that other forms do not.

In pushing back against the standardisation and conservatism entailed in traditional publishing, many scholar-led presses adopt much looser approaches to business models and how they influence the kinds of research published. Open Humanities Press describes "cost minimization rather than revenue generation" as a guiding principle, while Open Book Publishers equally claim to not be "fixated" on any business mode but sustain their efforts through a number of sources.[39] Presses such as Mayfly and Mattering report no ongoing institutional support, but they do receive small grants occasionally. While a mixture of practices are on display, between the completely do-it-yourself approach and more formalised attempts to generate revenue, none of the scholar-led presses have anything close to the large, formalised, salaried staff found in university presses and commercial publishers. This suggests a culture of resilience rather than one wedded to a unified, sustainable way of doing things; some of these presses are ephemeral and experimental in nature, and place diminished emphasis on long-term plans for sustainability.

Intimately bound up with the critique of commercial publishing and the standardisation it entails is a broader questioning of the practices and values within higher education itself. Many of the presses emphasised how higher education reinforces current publishing practices, particularly with respect to what "counts" as a publication—especially for career and funding purposes—and how this shapes humanities research. For example, Chris Land of MayFly Books argues against the "institutional forces that are delegitimising the project from the outset" through their requirement for publications from established presses.[40] Eileen Joy highlights how punctum books confronts this situation by giving legitimacy to "weird" publications:

> To have a press to literally promote the work that everybody wants to do but isn't allowed to do and yet, at the same time though, in order not to be just considered that fringe press over there that publishes the weird things that no one will give you credit for, for your national research exercise, at the same time we would surround the venture with the apparatus of a very legitimate press.[41]

Joy cites independent, avant-garde presses such as Semiotext(e) and Urbanomic as influences that maintain a high reputation in their fields while publishing "edgy, creative" work. punctum seeks to offer an OA outlet for this kind of work, along the lines of Derrida's idea of the "university without condition"—or "the principle right to say everything . . . and the right to say it publicly, to publish it."[42]

But the contemporary neoliberal university does have conditions. Many presses note a tension between critique and experimentation on the one hand and the need to conform to certain expectations of the university on the other. For Joy, it is "hard to balance" the desire to experiment with the need for legitimacy and sustainability. Similarly, Open Humanities Press aims to demonstrate the possibility of "high-profile, prestigious OA," while Mattering Press seeks to publish well-known scholars in order to gain a "high degree of credibility" so that early-career researchers will be able to publish with them, too. Counter Press seeks funding from its institution for the "impact" it demonstrates in exploring how law is "actually being applied in the world."[43] There is a need, therefore, for some new OA publishers to pragmatically conform to traditional standards around prestige, reputation, and impact, which will allow them to experiment in other areas.

This pragmatism is also reflected in the tension between theory and practice that necessarily arises in such endeavours. The academics who run each press are all scholars in the humanities and social sciences, ranging from permanently employed academics to precariously employed and para-academic researchers, and many see their publishing work as an extension of their scholarly work. MayFly Books speak of "politicising the business school in the sense of unpacking the power relations in our own institutional location [. . .]. I guess that fits with the project of academic publishing, where we can reflect on our own practice and then politicise that and do something differently."[44] Similarly, Eileen Joy (quoting Gary Hall of Open Humanities Press in the first line) writes:

> "How do you apply your theoretical principles to the structures that make your work visible?" Whether it is your university position, or your book: do you care about the machinations behind that? Where is your critique of the administrative bureaucracy of your own institution or of the institutions that publish your work? I have always felt that way myself, that if we are theorists, if we are radical, critical theorists, then our critique should aim at a transformation of the actual systems within which we work.[45]

So, for Joy, punctum books is a theory-led intervention into publishing that highlights and seeks to transform the "machinations" involved in knowledge production, be they the university, publishing, funding bodies, or something else.

As with the tension between theory and practice, the presses are forced to make decisions around when to adapt their ethical stance and when to adopt a more strategic approach. Each press has a remit, often one that is politically progressive, but it is forced to participate in certain practices that would not necessarily conform to this remit. It is not possible to be ideologically pure, especially when you must rely on commercial services such as Amazon for selling books and web-hosting, and Ingram Books for print-on-demand services. A number of presses remark on this as a source of frustration, but one that is unavoidable without a great deal of effort. Chris Land assert that using Amazon "kind of makes all of the political arguments I was trying to make earlier a bit rubbish."[46] Each press is forced to make a choice as to when it adopts a more pragmatic approach over an explicitly critical one.

But this pragmatism is itself a kind of political responsibility, the kind that is necessary for the possibility of any politics. Despite positioning themselves in opposition to the status quo of academic knowledge production, scholar-led presses are forced to make difficult decisions that may appear to conflict with their general ethico-political outlook, what Ernesto Laclau would term their "ethical investment."[47] This responsibility for making decisions is a feature of ethics and politics, following Derrida in particular. As Derrida writes: "A decision that didn't go through the ordeal of the undecidable would not be a free decision, it would only be the programmable application or unfolding of a calculable process."[48] Politics and ethics are always in progress, rather than a fixed project or plan to be rolled out, and so the scholar-led presses are continually making decisions about how to act on their critiques of the status quo, even if these decisions are difficult or have the appearance of a contradiction.

Care-full Publishing

Among the ethical commitments described by the presses interviewed, the notion of care occurs frequently as an important value guiding many of the scholar-led publishing programmes. Joe Deville articulates Mattering Press's interest in the ethics of care:

> That is the ethics we draw on in particular, because the press is interested in publishing works in and around Science and Technology Studies, and we have been quite influenced by the work of Annemarie Mol, who counterposes the logic of care to the logic of calculation. Annemarie Mol in part is also influenced by feminist work on care, and seeing care as where it was, attending to the relationality and the diverse forms of relationality that are being put into play with any practice really. As a Science and Technology Studies focussed publisher, we are also interested in what role non-human actors might play in mediating and shaping those relations of care. That is something that we are also attentive to.[49]

In the case of Mattering Press, care represents the intimate connection between STS theory and practice, illustrating that many of the presses implement ideas from their academic research into the way each press is run. But care and its related concepts, such as reciprocity, gift-giving, and codependence, are also helpful for theorising what sets scholar-led presses apart from other presses. The different approaches to and understandings of care are therefore worth exploring in some detail.

The ethics of care is a term deployed in a number of different disciplinary contexts to emphasise the relational and situated nature of ethics. From a feminist perspective, Joan Tronto famously defined care as "everything that we do to maintain, continue and repair 'our world' so that we can live in it as well as possible."[50] In opposition to more detached, rational, and liberal approaches to ethics, care involves focusing on maintenance and concern for the interdependence and embeddedness of humans and nonhumans within their worlds. But the ethical dimension of care, as María Puig de la Bellacasa shows, is not a normative moral obligation but instead concerns "thick, impure, involvement in a world where the question of how to care needs to be posed."[51] Care is messy and does not offer a roadmap for an ethico-political way of living; instead, it requires attentiveness to our environments and the collectives in which we participate. Care starts from the understanding that our existence in the world is dependent on others in a way that necessitates a responsible commitment to one another, even if (as per a deconstructive approach) the ethical content of this commitment is not determinable in advance. This understanding of subjectivity is in direct contrast to the individuating notions of subjectivity of the policymakers explored in the previous chapter.

Publishing is an inherently relational process involving a range of roles, from authors, reviewers, and editors to copyeditors, typesetters, and readers. Many of the presses understand the importance of care with respect to this relationality. Writing on their blog, the editors of Mattering Press argue how scholarship is benefitted by "open, productive collaboration" between authors, editors, and reviewers.[52] In encouraging open dialogue among these roles, particularly in the form of non-anonymous peer reviews, the press hopes to encourage a relationship of care between them all. The emphasis on open peer review as an exercise of care and relationship-building is distinct from traditional advocacy of open review originating largely in the sciences, which argues for its adoption because it increases accuracy and transparency, reduces delays and expense, and improves the paper through a "robust exchange of ideas."[53] Proponents of open review in the sciences also emphasise the credit that reviewers might receive for signing their review, conforming to the kinds of metricised cultures many of the scholar-led presses here seek to avoid. Mattering Press is unique, then, in valuing open review for the intrinsic, affective benefits of nurturing a relationship between author and reviewer.

In a similar vein, Open Humanities Press cites care work as important with respect to the labour involved in scholar-led publishing. OHP runs its operations through a decentralised network of working academics, who offer their labour as volunteers. This, they argue, is a way of decentering "waged work from its privileged place in neoliberal society and placing more emphasis on unwaged activities, including different kinds of carework."[54] Open Humanities Press provides a structure for academics to divert the labour they already gift to traditional commercial publishers (also at the expense of their copyright) to scholar-led presses. Many of the interviewed presses explicitly mention care of the volunteer labour they receive, particularly in not relying on the same volunteers continually and fairly treating "those without a direct stake in the distribution of the knowledge itself."[55] This is an extension of caring for the relationships involved in the publishing process. Each press is embedded in its own disciplinary network, and they recognise the value of fair treatment and reciprocity—e.g., Open Humanities Press specifically highlights how their knowledge and expertise is shared between other presses rather than kept as a proprietary secret.

In highlighting the relational nature of publishing practices, the employment of care as a guiding principle represents a move towards considerations of the community over the individual. This is a key facet of care, which represents a critique of liberal individualism by emphasising relationality and interdependence over rational detachment and calculation. For Annemarie Mol, care begins with humans as part of collectives (families, communities, relationships, etc.), and choice begins with individuals as customers who must take responsibility for their own choices.[56] The logic of choice is therefore detached and disinterested, ignoring the relational contexts in which people are situated (unlike care). Similarly, the logic of choice, in treating everyone the same, disproportionately favours majority groups, the wealthy, and those in a better position to influence their outcomes. There is also a normative dimension to the logic of choice, Mol argues, requiring that one ought to eat well and exercise, irrespective of one's situation, and one should take care of one's own choices of healthcare as an individual operating in the market. Care, on the other hand, focuses on "helpful differentiations" between the groups with which one associates oneself and lacks the strong normative dimension (as described above).[57]

Mol's notion of care, referenced by Mattering Press in the above quotation, is useful for understanding the values of the scholar-led OA presses, particularly in contrast to commercial forms of both closed and OA publishing that practice a "cookie cutter" approach described by punctum. For example, OA publishing achieved through article-processing charges can promote exactly this state of affairs, whereby publishers provide a particular service for a set fee—no more or less. In contrast, scholar-led presses tend to be embedded in their collectives, adopting a less outcomes-focused practice of scholarly communication and instead attending to the relational context of the work and its production. This is helped by the lack of focus on single, sustainable business models, which affords the flexibility to publish research in nonstandardised ways.

Care also extends to the works being published, the materiality of nonhuman actors in the publishing process. Many of the presses talk about ensuring that the published work is of high quality, in terms of either academic quality through the peer review and editing processes or in the finished publication through a professional production process. For Meson Press, care in the editing process is needed for academic rigour and for the press to be "taken seriously in the academic world."[58] Open Humanities Press aims to "show that it's perfectly possible to publish books especially open access, maintain high production standards, and achieve a certain level of prestige of the kind one gets from being associated with a traditional legacy print press when doing so."[59] Open Book Publishers takes care in the peer review process to match the academic quality of "the very best university presses."[60] Care here is synonymous with the kinds of legitimacy and quality expected by researchers of some traditional presses, particularly university presses.

Despite positioning themselves in opposition to many aspects of traditional publishing, a number of the presses referred to university press publishing as influential. Alongside Open Book Publishers referencing Cambridge University Press as a standard for quality, some of the presses explicitly valued the university press model for its academic oversight and ability to publish without pure commercial concerns. Chris Land of MayFly Books values the "strange, edgy, intermediary situation of the university presses," particularly smaller ones, over the "bigger commercial" university presses such as Oxford and Cambridge and those in the US. Smaller university presses are not simply led by commercial concerns, and as such offer a space for publishing that prioritises a logic of care over one of choice. This is perhaps why many of the presses speak favourably of university presses—punctum and MayFly Books both sought (unsuccessfully) to launch as formally affiliated presses with a university press designation, while Open Humanities Press partnered with Michigan Publishing at the University of Michigan Library for the first five years of its existence.

As a scholar-led university press, Goldsmiths Press was founded to regenerate "the traditions of the university press."[61] It is not immediately apparent what Sarah Kember, Director of Goldsmiths Press, means by this, but in a separate talk to launch Goldsmiths Press she refers to the "long tradition of publishing stuff that messes up the boundaries of arts and humanities."[62] Similarly, Chris Land hoped to relaunch the University of Leicester Press to leverage institutional resources and keep the press "under academic leadership within the university rather than having it as a kind of arm's length commercial spin-off."[63] In fact, OA has been particularly successful at regenerating the UK-based university press landscape, with a host of new OA university presses launched in the past decade, such as UCL Press, Westminster Press, the Scottish University Press, and the White Rose Press (a collaboration among Sheffield, York, and Leeds). Subsidised by their host institutions, these presses tend to focus on monograph publishing in humanities and social science disciplines, in many ways influenced by the North American university press landscape that was supported by host universities but is now increasingly forced to be self-sufficient. New university presses can afford to publish in ways that are not concerned with commercial returns, which in turn allows experimentation, the "strange" and "edgy," and the kinds of publications that are valued purely for scholarly reasons.

This ties neatly with the final usage of care I want to reference from the interviews, that of punctum's guiding principle of "care of the self." Borrowing from the title of volume 3 of Foucault's *The History of Sexuality*, Eileen Joy cites "care of the self" as one way to foster the kinds of experimentation that has "no regard whatsoever for outcomes or applications."[64] Foucault's exploration of care of the self relates to the idea that self-care, in the form of introspection, daily regimens, exercises, etc., was a foundational moral precept in ancient Greece.[65] Though it may appear individualistic when compared to those understandings of care explored so far, Foucault explains that care finds "ready support in the whole bundle of customary relations of kinship, friendship, and obligation."[66] Care of the self was inherently a community-based exercise for the ancients, Foucault shows, who had a right to receive guidance and counselling from others.

For Eileen Joy of punctum books, focusing on care of the self is a method of moving beyond mere critique and towards a transformation of the structures that force research into certain externally configured formats:

> punctum's guiding principles are that there is no way to know what the future of research is, without having a kind of open door that allows in the chimeric, the mad, the deviant, the improbable, the unforeseen and unanticipated modes. We shouldn't know in advance what we are doing. With every book proposal, when publishers ask you to propose a book, they have a format. They want you to know at the beginning

> where you are going to end up. They want you to say at the outset when you do a grant proposal, what the outcome will be. Everyone loathes that part of a grant proposal because they don't know the outcome of their research yet, but if they do not say they do know, they won't get the money. Therefore punctum feels that publishing is an art of care of the self, of the author, of their ideas, of their work.[67]

punctum seeks to provide a space for authors to explore their ideas for their intrinsic worth, rather than how they conform to certain expected "outcomes." Care here relates to experimentation and the absence of a need to conform, allowing authors to care solely for their research process rather than anything extraneous to it.

I have illustrated a number of different usages of care cited by the interviewed presses, particularly those relating to affect, ethics, and labour, and how an understanding of care helps elucidate the discourse and practices of each press. Though the various usages of the term come from different perspectives and disciplinary traditions, a thread running through each emphasises the relational and collective aspects of subjectivity and how this relates to the publishing process. Care offers a way to work through issues around labour, authorship, commercialism, and conservativism in publishing and research assessment. Scholar-led publishing is a way to reintroduce care to the publishing process through the freedom it affords for experimentation and nontraditional approaches to scholarship. This freedom also lends itself to cooperation rather than competition, and a sense of the collective over individualism. These aspects distinguish scholar-led publishing from the marketised forms of OA publishing that dominate the publishing landscape.

Scholar-Led OA and the Commons

In chapter 1, I argued that the relational labour of care is well conceived as a practice of commoning. Through the analysis of these scholar-led publishing projects, it is possible to see how care-full publishing works in practice and its relationship to the idea of the commons I am building within this book. As a form of care oriented around a specific shared resource, commoning provides the social relations for nonmarketised forms of production. It does this through informal practices of care, resilience, and shared enterprise within and across various institutional arrangements positioned towards a common(s) horizon. Commoning, for Massimo De Angelis, is the "source of grassroots power" against capital because of its ability to reproduce the social relations needed to allow more commons to flourish.[68] Under market-based systems of production, these social relations do exist but are extracted for and exploited by capital. This extraction is why the commons is a process of struggle between market and state forms of production, rather than being neatly separated from them.

The struggle of the hierarchy between market, state, and commons modes of production is clear within the work of scholar-led publishers. They are operating very much against the grain of neoliberal higher education, using their time and resources on publishing labours of love and not simply giving their free labour to the publishing industry. By materially supporting alternatives, the academics behind these projects contribute to a new ecology of commons-based publishing that foregrounds relational approaches over teleological market-based forms propped up by neoliberal governance. Nonetheless, although they are weaving a path between the market and state, scholar-led projects are not separate from them. The commons is not best conceived as a "third space" between market and state; rather, it is inextricably entangled with different modes of production. Presses reported having to make difficult and strategic decisions about which commercial services to work with to produce their publications. They are also beholden to various sources of funding predicated on the governmental support for OA that has freed up resources for a variety of OA projects. To this extent, scholar-led presses are "stealing" from the university, in the way that Harney and Moten described (discussed in the previous chapter), by exploiting the turn towards OA for their own ends.

There is a temptation, then, to view scholar-led publishing as prefigurative in the sense that it attempts to, as Guilherme Fians defines it, "build alternative futures in the present and to effect political change by not reproducing the social structures that activists oppose."[69] To an extent this is true, because many of the practices on display are a result of a rich imagination regarding the future of publishing and practices not currently supported within more traditional modes of publication. Yet there is a danger in viewing scholar-led publishing as prefigurative because universities might agree that *all* publishing can be undertaken by scholar collectives with little financial support. Scholar-led publishers are precarious and underresourced, and they have to teach themselves skills related to publishing and managing their operations. It is possible that, under the neoliberal logic of austerity, universities would begin to consider scholar-led publishing as *the* alternative to commercial models, without the need for additional support in terms of finance, time, and other forms of capacity-building. This neoliberal promotion of commons-based self-management is a way of withdrawing rather than offering support to publishing communities; it is a frequent strategy for capitalist actors when confronting the commons, as when the World Bank promoted self-reliance in order to remove state funding from local communities in rural locations.[70] The scholar-led commons must be a site of struggle both for itself and for the external forms of support and legitimation it needs from institutions and the state. The labour for scholar-led publishing should therefore be valued by and within the institution, as a form of service to one's scholarship and disciplinary communities, as Janneke Adema and I have argued previously.[71]

So, rather than viewing scholar-led publishing as a model that can be used to replace commercial journals, a better way to see it, as Janneke Adema does, is as a form of affirmative critique:

> For these projects, experimenting is very much an affirmative speculative practice, a means to reperform our existing scholarly institutions and practices in potentially more ethical and responsible ways; opening up spaces for otherness and differentiation beyond our hegemonic conceptual knowledge frameworks; and exploring more inclusive forms of knowledge, open to ambivalence and failure.[72]

Scholar-led publishing is an extension of academic work and a performative approach to reimagining publishing. It is both generative and experimental in its practice, meaning it cannot be easily standardised. The work of scholar-led publishers therefore needs to be financially supported within universities as valuable in itself, and not because it might allow us to ease university budgets and push all the labour for publishing onto working academics.

Perhaps it is possible to frame the affirmative critique of scholar-led publishing in terms of what Chantal Mouffe calls a "counter-hegemonic challenge" to the dominant publishing culture.[73] We have already seen from Eileen Joy that scholar-led presses attempt to move beyond mere critique into "a transformation of the actual systems within which we work." Their existence is itself an example of pushing back against the dominant cultures of OA, and of publishing more broadly, through both practice-based and discursive means. And though the presses are not united by any specific philosophy or approach, they are best theorised as embodying critique of the current systems of publishing in the humanities. Scholar-led publishers form a counter-hegemonic challenge to the current dominant modes of publishing similar to those undertaken by other grassroots artistic and cultural communities. In an essay entitled "Agonistic Politics and Artistic Practices," Mouffe describes the various practices and discourses artists employ to change the dominant conception of reality, what Gramsci termed the "common sense."[74] Through a series of cultural and artistic (not traditionally "political") practices, counter-hegemonic interventions aim to create the possibility of new subjectivities in civil society. Mouffe uses the example of Alfredo Jaar's artistic work that poses simple questions in public places in order to "trigger reflections that will arouse discontent with the current state of things."[75] As an "aesthetics of resistance," Mouffe highlights Jaar's work (and the presence of subversive art more generally) for its affective potential in constructing new forms of subjectivity based on positing alternatives and new possibilities. It is possible to consider scholar-led publishing in a similar way.

The affective potential of disruptive publishing practices is one way that scholar-led presses unsettle dominant ideas around publishing. Making publications openly available, born-digital, and not for profit is one way to highlight why these ideas are subversive and why the scholar-led presses felt the need to take responsibility for publishing themselves. We can thus think of scholar-led publishing, following Mouffe, as a series of "counter-hegemonic interventions whose objective is to disrupt the smooth image that corporate capitalism tries to spread."[76] Scholar-led presses represent the existence of alternatives that can resist commercialised publishing and point to new forms of organisation. It is clear how, coupled with traditional discursive forms of advocacy, such a strategy could begin to change the common sense around publishing. One of the main reasons OA policies will not have this effect, I contend, is that they are based in compliance and mandates, not on encouraging engagement through new forms of praxis. In fact, the affective potential of OA policies might actually be the feature that works against the adoption of critical publishing practices through the association that OA is punitive rather than based in freedom.

But Mouffe also discusses how counter-hegemonic strategies need to engage with—not withdraw from—the institutions that maintain the dominant hegemony. Withdrawing from institutional attachments implies that art and culture can only be understood outside the institutional context, and ignores the "multiplicity of avenues that are open for political engagement."[77] In the case of scholar-led presses, this means employing various strategies to engage with the university, funders, and governments to undermine the dominant ideological framework. A good example of this is Goldsmiths Press, which operates within the university and in the service of Goldsmiths' theoretical and artistic commitments. Many of the presses interviewed had a positive view of university presses, and the need to bring publication practices inside the university as a way to reclaim them from commercial publishers, despite the university's complicity in "commercialisation, standardisation and audit," as Sarah Kember describes.[78] This engagement again recognises that the commons is inseparable from the market and the state, and that continual engagement is needed with each mode of production and the institutions that represent them.

Having explored the dominant themes around scholar-led forms of publishing, I am now turning more explicitly to this question of support and influence for alternative approaches to publishing. As we have seen, scholar-led publishers are atomised and precarious, often relying on limited money and time while trying to learn a variety of technical and editorial processes. The next chapter explores questions of scale and infrastructure for the publishing commons, guided by the desire to support alternative projects without erasing their locality and difference.

Chapter 4

Infrastructuring the Open Access Publishing Commons

I began chapter 1 of this book with a discussion of the acquisition by Elsevier of bepress, a commercial academic software firm that owns the Digital Commons repository and publishing service used by many universities in North America and elsewhere. While the name Digital Commons reveals a great deal about the usage of the term "commons" by commercial organisations, the acquisition of bepress also illustrates something pernicious about the strategies of large commercial publishing houses and the end-to-end publishing workflows they are seeking to own and monetise. Elsevier no longer describes itself as a publisher, but as a "global information analytics company" due to its increasing focus on capturing and processing data to sell insights into a range of academic and research sectors. bepress represents one component in a growing portfolio of acquisitions by Elsevier designed to facilitate ownership of the entire knowledge-production life cycle, which also includes the purchases of the reference manager Mendeley, the disciplinary repository SSRN, the editorial management software company

Aries, the analytics suite Plum, the research performance service SciVal, and many others. This trend towards owning the research life cycle is not unique to Elsevier; it is a notable feature of the consolidated academic publishing landscape, as Alejandro Posada and George Chen note in an influential paper on the ownership of infrastructure by commercial publishers.[1]

The totalising approach to the research life cycle now defines the evolution of commercial research infrastructures. Publishers seek to control this life cycle in order to fence individual researchers within the walled gardens they create, thus allowing maximum opportunities to profit from their content and behaviour. This strategy marks a shift, from publishers as providers of content to providers of services for researchers within their centrally controlled ecosystems. I have theorised this elsewhere as a process of *individuation through infrastructure* whereby researchers are further atomised into individual, traceable, measurable units by commercial research infrastructures, which opens them up to deeper and more granular forms of assessment by research institutions and funders.[2] In doing this, publishers are focused more on infrastructures that automate and nudge researchers, providing tools for them to share more research and user data, or to provide more information that further locks in their workflows and processes. Roger Schonfeld has theorised this publisher-driven process as creating "supercontinents" within which all content is served up for researchers in a seamless way.[3] Taking the consolidation of publishing into account too, this conception of future supercontinents of scholarly publishing, dominated by a handful of commercial organisations battling for individual researchers, is quite persuasive—and pernicious.

The move to individuation also has surveillant capabilities, as Sarah Lamdan illustrates through her research on analytics firms such as RELX (the owners of Elsevier), Thomson Reuters, and Clarivate. Lamdan explores how tracking researchers through publisher "walled gardens" has ordering implications for academic behaviour:

> Combining research with data analytics doesn't just hurt research, it also hurts the researchers themselves. Data companies' algorithms can determine who gets jobs. Hiring and tenure committees rely on impact metrics to measure scholars' value, using the data products to determine scholars' career trajectories. Metrics weigh so heavily in hiring choices that they change how scholars spend their time.[4]

Coupling the supercontinent idea with the increasing surveillance of academic publishers and institutions helps us see, following Nick Couldry and Gabriel Mejias, how infrastructure is now being designed in a way that "colonises" user and research data.[5] Publishers do this to amass as much data as possible, to sell on to other analytics firms or to analyse and use to build services. Data colonialism is, for Couldry and Mejias, neoliberalism taken to its logical conclusion: opening up ("literally annexing") all areas of life to monetisation as data.[6] It is an exercise of power that makes the individual wholly available to capital, resulting in the "degradation" of life through continual surveillance. This is the infrastructural world being developed as the publishing market shifts towards open access and seeks additional revenue in the process through user lock-in. The strategy is totalising, homogenising, automated, and extractive of research communities.

But what would it take for the kinds of publishers discussed in the previous chapter to thrive within and in opposition to this environment? How is it possible to support a bibliodiverse ecosystem of researcher-led presses and their associated infrastructures—the commons I have been arguing for in this book—especially when the publishing world is moving in the opposite direction? This is the question I hope to answer in this chapter.

It is tempting to want to position alternative forms of scholar-led publishing as a direct challenge to commercial forms of OA publishing. Scholar-led publishing is better, more ethical, and should therefore seek to supersede the commercial publishing hegemony through a seamless transition from commercial to scholar-led. Scholar-led publishing is precarious and underfunded, so there must be a way to redirect material resources away from bad actors towards good actors. For example, Pia et al. see scholar-led publishing as a way to "fight back" against commercial publishing by rewarding a "fairer" set of publication choices and practices that lead to the "de-commercialisation of academic publishing.[7] While these are good aims, they will have limited impact on the commercial makeup of the publishing industry, which is heavily skewed towards commercialisation and able to co-opt any schemes to fix it. Part of the problem with advocating for systemic change is that it naturally leads to grand, homogenising thinking at the expense of ideas about small, situated, and careful routes forward.

A similar argument for systemic change is made in many calls for a diamond OA future in which all research is immediately made freely accessible without payment by authors or readers. For example, the Science Europe and cOAlition S "OA

Diamond Journals Study" aimed to gain a "better understanding" of the OA diamond landscape, including the opportunities, challenges, and pathways to non-APC-based publishing.[8] The study made a number of recommendations aimed ultimately at a "unified, interconnected and interoperable OA diamond infrastructure and offering." One is to create an OA diamond "capacity centre" that would provide advice and technical support for diamond journals, particularly designed to allow them to build "technical, editorial, financial and administrative capacity." The proposal for the capacity centre subsequently found a home in the EU-funded project Developing Institutional Open Access Publishing Models to Advance Scholarly Communication (DIAMAS). Here, the emphasis is on how to best organise the work of diamond journals through toolkits, specific standards, guidelines, training materials, and business model canvasses.[9] Ultimately, the aim is to professionalise diamond journals to allow them to form a coherent alternative to commercial publishing options, an aim also implicitly shared in the European Council's call for nonprofit, "no pay" publishing in place of the article-processing charge.[10]

The aims of DIAMAS and Science Europe are laudable regarding the move towards diamond forms of open access and its potential to influence scholarly publishing more generally. Yet to make a convincing case that community-led forms of OA publishing can undermine the commercial publishing hegemony, advocates are also forced to replicate commercial logic and argue for various forms of standardisation and professionality that work against both experimentation and bibliodiversity. This foreclosure of possibilities is inherent in systemic approaches to change that seek "global alignment" and require that one dominant model be replaced with another.[11] These grand ambitions are also a prerequisite for material support by funders, universities, and other powerful actors looking for ways to intervene and shape a particular outcome, which is why they must appear politically neutral and not be seen to disrupt the fundamental idea of publishing as a commercial activity. It is noteworthy, for example, that the Science Europe study aims to develop an "organised marketplace" for diamond OA publishing, rehearsing the language of commercial models.[12]

Clearly, there are strategic reasons to adopt a position that what you are developing will have a major impact on dominant ways of doing things. The impact agenda is well known and influences much of how funding is applied for and distributed, especially in areas relating to policymaking, and requires academics to tailor their applications to highlight their *broad societal impacts*.[13] This situation reveals the bind that advocates of radical forms of open access find themselves in: on the one hand, needing to propose a grand plan to tackle the problems with commercial publishing, while on the other hand understanding that grand plans necessarily undermine their own objectives of small, careful, relational forms of publishing that do not have a self-defined tangible goal. But, as the authors of the "After Open Access" manifesto write:

> Publishing after open access does not have a resolution (let alone a technological solution) or endpoint, but rather is a continual process of discussion, controversy-making and opening up to possibilities. We do not know what journal publishing after open access is, but we do know that we must work together in order to create a just alternative to the exist-

> ing extractive and predatory model, an alternative that operates according to a different set of values and priorities than those that dominate scholarly publishing at the moment. These values and priorities need to inform or constitute new publishing systems committed to the public ownership rather than the continued privatization of knowledge.[14]

Rather than attempting to standardise and professionalise alternative forms of OA publishing, the "After Open Access" authors—themselves a "collective of feminist and social justice editors"—argue for the need to experiment and open publishing up to possibilities. This "opening up" is a recognition of the fact that ethical approaches to publishing resist standardisation through the mechanics of commercialisation and instead need to be built on structures that avoid resolution and foreground experimentation.

This chapter explores a variety of attempts to build and nurture the structures, or more specifically the infrastructures, to support alternative forms of OA publishing beyond the values of the market. In doing so, it looks to a number of approaches that take as their starting point the desire to make alternative, diverse forms of OA resilient without homogenising their practices through economies of scale. Through these initiatives, I begin to illustrate how OA publishing can be achieved without recourse to brute marketisation and by nurturing commons-based projects based on alternative infrastructural logics.

For the late theorist Lauren Berlant, the concept of the commons is best deployed in nurturing infrastructures for "troubling times."[15] The commons is not a solution to these times, and Berlant "holds in suspicion" the current academic popularity of the term, which, they argue, often reflects a vision that "merely needs the world to create infrastructures to catch up to it." Instead, for Berlant, the commons allows us to "point to a way to view what's broken in sociality, the difficulty of convening a world conjointly, although it is inconvenient and hard, and to offer incitements to imagining a liveable provisional life."[16] The commons, then, is about sociality—i.e., the different ways of getting and being together—and *not* about how to roll out a set of infrastructures for supporting our predetermined, fixed understanding of how communities behave and get along.

Following Berlant, I want to foreground this idea of sociality as integral to the work of supporting scholar-led publishing through infrastructures that permit different kinds of collective experimentation. By infrastructure, however, I mean something more than just the technical forms of physical or digital support structures. Infrastructure is *socio*-technical: it is wholly dependent on communities of people whose work is often invisible as part of their practice of maintenance and care. Indeed, as Susan Leigh Star writes, infrastructure is itself invisible until it "breaks down" and its absence reveals what is now missed.[17] This means that much of the work of infrastructure, for Star, goes "unnoticed" or is "not formally recognised."[18] This work is inherently connected to the informal repertoires of communities of practice and the nuanced ways of working that make infrastructural usage inexplicably linked to the identities of individual communities. Infrastructures therefore facilitate, and are facilitated by, different kinds of socialities, gatherings, and belongings. They are used differently by different communities—they are "relational," as Star puts it—and as such can never be divorced from the actors who use them.

While many arguments about OA claim that publishing is principally an infrastructural issue, they fail to adequately account for this social dimension and instead foreground the platforms, software, and other technical elements that contribute to the production of academic publications.[19] This tendency emphasises a universalising understanding of scholarly communication infrastructures, rather than their embeddedness in particular localities and individual communities. Such an infrastructural "view from nowhere" is severely limiting in its promotion of a homogeneous infrastructural landscape, one that is particularly susceptible to the business objectives of commercial providers such as Elsevier, discussed above.

Yet, as the media theorist Jonathan Gray illustrates, scholarly communication is the perfect area for infrastructural experimentations and interventions that do not presuppose homogeneity. Gray writes, "infrastructures do not only facilitate access to preexisting publics, they can also gather their own."[20] They do this by drawing together different communities in previously unexplored ways based on alternative logics that "reflect, enact, and configure" how research is made public. What follows is an exploration of the interplay between scale and heterogeneity as evidenced by approaches to open-access infrastructures that move beyond the totalising logics of marketisation.

The Radical Open Access Collective

Formed in 2015, the Radical Open Access Collective (ROAC) is a loose global collective of OA presses in the humanities and social sciences, all entirely organised and maintained by working academics. The collective consists of over eighty members, who publish a range of books, journals, and experimental works, from fully professional typeset productions published with regularity to entirely DIY processes and lo-fi outputs published sporadically. None of the presses in the collective charge APCs. Instead, projects are funded by a range of sources and mixed models, including grants, university support, and other in-kind contributions, but they are sustained primarily by labour gifted by academics and redirected from commercial publishing efforts. In doing so, ROAC members represent an approach to publishing that is less reliant on the market and is instead led entirely by research communities themselves.[21] I and my colleagues Janneke Adema, Rebekka Kiesewetter, and Toby Steiner are currently "co-organisers" of the collective, though in practice far more people are involved in sustaining the collective in various capacities. The ROAC is guided by a philosophy of promoting experimentation, ethics of care, critiques of the status quo, underrepresented cultures of knowledge, and noncommercial approaches to publishing.[22]

Many of the scholar-led presses and journals discussed in the previous chapter are members of the collective; so too are African Minds, Cadernos de Linguística, Culture Machine, Minor Compositions, and Tuwhera. The collective strives to represent and support the global diversity of scholar-led publishing projects from scholars at all career levels. This involves nurturing cultures of knowledge associated with spaces that are "outside" the walls of the university as they are conventionally conceived, as well as ensuring that para-academics, precariously employed scholars, and those living outside the global North and West are all able to have a voice. Forms of collectivity need to include this diversity in their modes of organization, and a number of models are on display in the collective that support these aims in various ways.

Despite the clear preference for nonprofit publishing, member presses and projects range from those with formalized models for revenue generation and sustainability, such as Open Book Publishers and punctum books, to completely DIY approaches with little to no financial support or commercial orientation, such as MayFly Books and Roving Eye Press, who instead rely solely on small grants and gifted labour for their projects. Many member projects are situated within and/or scaffold upon a university setting, such as the Institute of Network Cultures and Goldsmiths Press, while others act as disparate networks of scholars with a wide range of locations and institutional attachments. As a noncompetitive and nonhierarchical collective, these differing levels of support and institutional attachment offer opportunities to share expertise and knowledge on successful (and unsuccessful) experiments in our various projects. This collaboration ensures that members can learn from one another's experiences and not continually reinvent wheels in isolation, unlike in private forms of publishing in which commercial knowledge is proprietary and "commercially sensitive."

Part of being a heterogeneous collective means that members experiment with a variety of practices and forms of publishing. Journals such as *Vectors*, *Thresholds*, and *Textshop Experiments* publish experimental, innovative, and hybrid works that confront traditional notions of paper-centric publishing and seek to fully explore and utilize the potential of digital environments for new forms of readership and textuality. Other projects attempt to engage with traditional and taken-for-granted understandings of contemporary academic practices. Projects such as Humanities Commons experiment with notions of academic social media self-branding, in opposition to for-profit, data-driven companies such as ResearchGate and Academia.edu, while the *Journal of Peer Production* and the *Public Philosophy Journal* operate nonstandard forms of peer review with a view to making the process more collegial and less focused on the evaluative and gatekeeping aspects of scholarly review. Many of these practices strive to reorient publishing as a form of care—care for others, for processes, for the work involved in all aspects of the supply chain, and for the (content of the) publication—rather than being focused purely on the outcomes of the publishing process.

The collective also represents a number of projects that prioritize a variety of audiences, authors, and global publics in their publishing practices. El Consejo Latinoamericano de Ciencias Sociales itself represents a collective of publishers from Latin America, the Caribbean, and beyond, aiming to "promote social research to combat poverty and inequality, strengthen human rights and democratic participation." Presses such as Éditions Science et Bien Commun, sdvig press, and African Minds represent communities outside the global North and West, each offering a reminder that OA publishing should represent the voices of diverse communities. In a similar way, members such as Mattering Press, Capacious, and the *Public Philosophy Journal* aim to support and bring to the fore the work of early-career researchers, who themselves have historically had a fraught relationship with OA publishing practices.

The global composition of this group, alongside the precarious and DIY nature of its presses, means that the ROAC exists to foster collaboration and mutual reliance over the competition and atomisation promoted by neoliberal cultures of higher education. Presses therefore rely on each other for advice and to share resources, while some promote each other's work at conferences and build smaller formalised collectives within the collective of like-minded presses, such as the ScholarLed consortium and the Free Journals Network—the boundaries of the collective are porous rather than solid. The ROAC facilitates a different kind of social publishing infrastructure based on informal alliances and happenstance connections, emphasising the relationalities and connections within this grassroots publishing ecology.

The ROAC therefore aims to do things differently and offer an alternative infrastructural scaffolding for projects that do not simply conform to commercialisation. As Janneke Adema writes:

> Focused on experimentation and the exploration of new institutions, relationalities, and practices, this approach toward openness, examining new formats and stimulating sharing and reuse of content as part of a knowledge commons, can be seen as a radical alternative to, and critique of, the business ethics underlying innovations in the knowledge economy.[23]

A nonteleological approach to openness—i.e., one without a presupposed destination—facilitates publishing practices that can undermine the commercial imperative and show other scholars how they can do it too. The ROAC therefore institutionalises the kinds of exploratory practices that commercial institutions tend to inhibit due to their need for economies of scale and easily replicable, labour-saving publishing practices. It does this by nurturing cultures of mutual reliance as the glue that holds together the collective—and scholar-led publishing.

Elsewhere, Janneke Adema and I have theorised the work of the ROAC as promoting a kind of *latent commons*, following Anna Lowenhaupt Tsing's terminology, which is an informal site of sharing in the service of loose affiliation between like-minded parties.[24] The latent commons is a place where, as Tsing writes, "entanglements might be mobilized in common cause."[25] It is not a formalised institution, a jointly managed common-pool resource in the sense of Elinor Ostrom and many other commons theorists; rather, it is a space of interaction with other like-minded collaborators that is completely informal in its makeup. No rules or formalised procedures govern the actions within the latent commons—everything is left to shared, normative cultures, good will, and what Tsing terms "effervescence"—the energy of the interactions. The ROAC is a latent commons in this sense. It is not a formal alliance between presses, nor is it a central location for the sharing of resources, but it promotes a kind of mutual reliance that holds the collective together and positions it as a distinct model of scholarly publishing. One might also draw on Harney and Moten's "undercommons" to describe the ROAC's fugitive hospitality.[26] It exists within the university as a space for coming together and helping each other out, but is also not formally recognised by the university and in many ways exists despite (and in opposition to) the university's commercial and individuating tendencies.

Many of these individuating tendencies are displayed through the OA policymaker preference for Creative Commons licensing that reinforces individual ownership of scholarly material. CC BY is the default licence for OA policies such as Plan S, which allows people to reuse material as long as the original author is cited as the creator of the work. The individuating feature of CC licensing works against a latent commons of shared, non-ownable resources, leading other radical OA projects to explore alternative arrangements for sharing intellectual work. The Collective Conditions for Reuse (CC4r) project attempts to reimagine CC licenses for collective non-ownership of creative resources. The legal deed states, "The authored work released under the CC4r was never yours to begin with. The CC4r considers authorship to be part of a collective cultural effort and rejects authorship as ownership derived from individual genius."[27] While CC4r distances itself from the legalistic language of licensing, their approach is similar to that of other free culture licences, with the crucial distinction that reusers are encouraged to take the "implications of their appropriation into account" and ground their reuse in the idea that authorship is a profoundly collective endeavour, thus decentring the individual, proprietorial subject in favour of the collective.

Nevertheless, just as this collective work within the latent commons does not "institutionalise well," as Tsing writes, so too is the ROAC limited in its ability to enact cultural change within academic publishing. Some degree of formality and institutionalisation is required to expand the possibilities of scholar-led publishing and make it less precarious, but the aim is to do so without homogenising the diversity and locality of the presses that make up the collective. The idea of "scaling small" becomes a way to build this resilience through collaboration and without recourse to marketisation.

Scaling Small and Boundary Commoning

The Radical Open Access Collective is a site for preserving and expanding bibliodiversity. Presses in the collective represent a tangled web of different publishing practices in terms of form, language, subject matter, and style, precisely because they are not required to conform to market norms. Rebekka Kiesewetter defines bibliodiversity as:

> [T]he linguistic, cultural, methodological, and epistemic diversity of academic content and output, both on national and international levels. It emphasises the need for a variety of publications to be available to readers within a specific environment (for example, academia) and the importance of publishers and journal editors in fostering such a diversity. Within the for-profit logic in a part of the academic publishing sphere, the predominance of a few big commercial publishers, the dominance of English language publications, and humanism-centred writing standards as a main reference for academic writing—bibliodiversity is under threat.[28]

Bibliodiversity is under threat due to consolidation within academic publishing, in part driven by commercial models for OA that seek the greatest return for minimum costs. Bibliodiverse publishing requires the recognition of care and human expertise and so does not flourish well under commercial models of publishing, particularly those driven by automation and high prestige, where the brand is more important than the final publication. The dominance of English in academic publishing is also a function of industry concentration that finds no monetary reward in multilingualism.[29]

The informality of the ROAC helps facilitate a bibliodiverse culture by not imposing particular economic, linguistic, or epistemological models onto publishing. Yet this informality also works against the possibility of larger-scale change, even though this is not the ROAC's intention, precisely because a certain degree of scale is required to be able to effect change. Though the ROAC is valuable in itself, it is also important to explore other avenues of making change through strategic alliance-building. Examples include collaborations involving libraries, universities, funding agencies, and infrastructure providers, all with a shared interest in the public value of knowledge. Here, there is scope for thinking of the various not-for-profit entities in scholarly communication as potential community partners in the emerging OA commons of academic publishing. The aim, then, becomes to realign the existing resources in the system of academic publishing, and to direct them to alternative not-for-profit collaborative models.

For Anna Lowenhaupt Tsing, scaling or scalability assumes that projects expand smoothly without changing their framing assumptions. For example, in a business context this refers to a firm's ability to expand without changing the nature of what it does or without changing its organisation. Economies of scale would comprise one such kind of business scalability.[30] The aim is to make projects more scalable for expansion—for growth, profit, and progress—and the desirability for doing so is taken for granted, Tsing argues. In other words, to scale up or to scale well implies developing the quality called "scalability," which is the ongoing ability to expand without changing. Yet it is important to emphasise that the intention here is not only to improve but also to naturalise scalability. According to Tsing, this illustrates how the discourse of scaling up has been strongly connected to our ideas of progress and to the advancement of humanity, where the success of expansion through scalability has shaped both modernity and capitalism—and with them, knowledge production. From this perspective, a system that is sustainable ought to be scalable, and nonscalable systems become an impediment to progress.

The issue with scalable projects, as Tsing points out, is that they tend to be oblivious both to the diversity of contexts and to the indeterminacies that originate from encounters with this diversity. Scalability allows us to see only uniform blocks, ready for further expansion, blocking our ability to notice the heterogeneity of the world and disguising its divisions. As Tsing explains:

> Scalability is possible only if project elements do not form transformative relationships that might change the project as elements are added. But transformative relationships are the medium for the emergence of diversity. Scalability projects banish meaningful diversity, which is to say, diversity that might change things.[31]

The urge for scalability has transformed both our societies and our landscapes—and similarly our knowledge systems and infrastructures—but it hasn't been able to suppress nonscalable economic and ecological relationships, which continue to erupt in unexpected places.[32] Yet Tsing does not see the nonscalable as existing in a normative relationship to scalability here (i.e., as one being good and the other being bad). The main distinguishing feature between scalable and nonscalable projects is not ethical conduct; it is, rather, that the latter are more diverse because they are not geared up for expansion. Scalability banishes meaningful diversity, that is, diversity that might change things.

How, then, does the scholar-led publishing commons scale without banishing this meaningful diversity? The answer lies in a particular approach to commoning that I and my collaborator Janneke Adema have termed "scaling small."[33] This principle eschews standard approaches to organisational growth that tend to flatten community diversity through economies of scale. Instead, scaling small puts forward the idea that scale can be nurtured through intentional collaborations between community-driven projects that promote a robust but bibliodiverse ecosystem of publishing. In this way, projects knit themselves together through their social interactions and their shared commitment to more radical approaches to publishing (and beyond). Unlike for-profit ecosystems in which larger commercial providers seek to acquire and incorporate smaller companies, much as Elsevier is doing with its approach to infrastructure, scaling small presupposes that smallness is worth preserving and so cannot be subsumed into a larger totalising project.

Part of the inspiration of scaling small comes from the commons theorist Massimo De Angelis and his idea of "boundary commoning." For De Angelis, boundary commoning is quite literally the "commoning that crosses boundaries, activates and sustains relations among commons thus giving shape to commons at larger scales."[34] It does this by opening up the boundaries of commons-based projects towards those of other commons-based projects, creating what De Angelis refers to as "structural coupling." Instead of persisting as distinct entities, these projects become more interdependent in how they both welcome and rely on others as part of their work. But crucially, boundary commoning depends on the necessity of boundaries because, as De Angelis writes, "commons are not open access but involve some community working out, governing and defining the rules of access."[35] This returns us to the original theorisation of the commons as inherently about community sociality. So, for our purposes, while the *outputs* of OA publishers are freely accessible to all (along with other associated resources), the necessity of preserving locality and bibliodiversity requires certain boundaries, so that communities may govern their own work. This does not mean communities are based on naive exclusivity, but rather that the idea of community—and thus the commons—only makes sense with respect to some kind of structure or boundary, however porous.

Scaling small draws on the idea of boundary commoning as part of its overall theory of change in academic publishing. It recognises that political change is not about replacing one broken system with another predetermined one; it is instead a continual and unfinishable process of experimentation and alliance-making within many overlapping systems and actors. Publishing industry commentators fail to appreciate the strategic dynamics of what many proponents for OA and ethical forms of publishing are trying to achieve. For example, the longstanding chronicler of open access Richard Poynder writes, "if the goal is to achieve universal open access then OA advocates might seem to have little choice but to think in terms of all-encompassing global and industrial initiatives, rather than cottage industries."[36] This kind of logic simply rehearses the commercial understanding of publishing and plays into the hands of those who control the conditions for "all-encompassing global and industrial initiatives."

I hope I have shown so far that OA itself, at least my conception of it, is about far more than mere "universal open access," but instead requires us to engage with the conditions of how academic knowledge is produced and disseminated, something that commercial models are not able to appreciate in their orientation around profit. Or rather, *openness* itself requires us to reassess and experiment with these conditions of publishing; it does not simply refer to universal access to academic knowledge. OA should be seen, as Janneke Adema writes, "not as a homogeneous project striving to become a dominating model or force; not as a thing, an object, or a model with prescribed meaning or ideology; but as a project with an unknown outcome, as an ongoing series of critical struggles. And this is exactly why we cannot pin down open (nor radical open access) as a concept, but instead need to leave it open: open to otherness and difference, and open to adapt to different circumstances."[37]

Scaling small offers a complication of this false binary between "global and industrial initiatives" and "cottage industries" and puts forward an approach to openness that allows these critical struggles to flourish. It does so by bringing together like-minded projects and institutions to collaborate on infrastructural development and collective models to support their activities. Through this approach, projects maintain their distinct local identities as they develop resilient, global structures to support their work. Scaling small is more formalised than the happenstance informality of the Radical Open Access Collective and so benefits from the scale that larger structures can generate. However, it also requires more coordination and genuine attempts to work together in an otherwise competitive funding environment. The formality of this kind of collaboration means that governance is a key consideration to ensure fairness and reciprocity and that conflicts can be adequately resolved.

The Community-led Open Publishing Infrastructures for Monographs (COPIM) project is guided by the philosophy of scaling small.[38] Funded by UK Research and Innovation (UKRI, the national funding body of the UK) and the Arcadia Foundation, the COPIM Project is a multistakeholder consortium designing collaborative and innovative models for OA book publishing, particularly those that support an ecosystem of small, noncommercial presses aligned with the COPIM philosophy. It brings together not just publishers, but technology providers, libraries, and infrastructure services, all in the service of preserving and nurturing bibliodiverse cultures of book publishing. For example, the project team designed the Open Book Collective, an approach to funding OA books that brings together libraries and publishers and acts as an intermediary organisation between them. Libraries can choose to pay relatively small amounts of money to support small presses in their pursuit of open access books. This ensures that OA books do not have to seek a market return through print sales and allows noncommercial approaches to flourish. The COPIM project went to great lengths to design robust systems of governance that all members can participate in, ensuring that no one organisation can make a decision without community support.[39]

In another approach by COPIM, the Opening the Future initiative supports OA monographs by providing a platform that allows libraries to subscribe to published backlists in order to make the frontlists (newly published titles) OA.[40] This model has been adopted by Liverpool University Press and the Central European University Press, and is also being replicated by MIT Press and the University of Michigan Press. The model is premised on the idea that libraries need to provide a budgetary justification for supporting OA books—i.e., that they get something in return—and so uses this transactional nature of publishing to make forthcoming titles available to everyone. The model only works if libraries and publishers are seen as collaborators rather than customers and producers, thus seeking to reset the traditional values system on which marketised publishing is based. In undermining the transactional approach to book publishing, the model permits so-called free riders who cannot afford to contribute but still benefit from openly available content.

Finally, from a technical perspective, COPIM seeks to provide the infrastructural support for open-source metadata management through its Thoth platform.[41] This service responds to commercial cultures of book cataloguing and distribution that prioritise sales as the way books enter library systems. Such systems work against noncommercial, nonanglophone, OA publishing by forcing all books through the same commercial systems owned by a handful of multinational publishers. Thoth provides a well-resourced open-source alternative to commercial metadata standards and workflows, something particularly attractive to libraries looking to catalogue OA books in the same way as toll-access books in order to not present them as second-class objects.

COPIM's mission and aims align with those of similar community-led projects, cooperatives, and collectives in other regions and language localities, most notably OPERAS, Humanities Commons, AmeliCA, the ROAC, CLACSO, African Journals Online, and Redalyc, all developing not-for-profit, open, and scholar-led knowledge systems and infrastructures. Throughout these initiatives runs a strong thread of need for intentionally designed governance procedures to support their work, something that is antagonistic to market-led projects and frequently an afterthought for community-led projects that rely on goodwill rather than explicitly detailed rules and governance structures. Humanities Commons, a nonprofit infrastructure providing spaces for scholarly communities to interact and share their work, has an extensive list of web pages on their governance procedures and how they sustain their work, declaring "We're not only building the Commons—we're documenting our work to sustain it."[42] The initiative outlines the various boards and councils that oversee its work, along with their bylaws, vision, purpose, and financial details. Populating their advisory boards with members of other collectives and projects working towards more ethical forms of scholarly communication is also a form of scaling small, embedding like-minded people within each other's projects (structural coupling). Working in a higher education system so beholden to competition, COPIM seeks to foster collaboration with other projects, aiming to carefully nurture shared publishing futures through cooperation and the promotion of diverse cultures of knowledge. Coupled with experimentation in the latent commons of the ROAC, new collaborative approaches to scaling represent the possibilities of more resilient forms of scholar-led academic publishing.

Scaling Small and the Knowledge Commons

The infrastructural experimentation of projects like the COPIM project, guided by the philosophy of scaling small, will not "fix" OA publishing, nor will it turn commercial forms of publishing into a harmonious commons. Indeed, the stakeholders involved are all still beholden to the economic constraints that beset higher education under neoliberal capitalism. This means they are still required to compete with one another in certain ways, despite being in favour of more cooperative forms of organisation. Scaling small is not a fix to OA publishing because, as I have stressed throughout, no such fix exists. However, in returning to the original conception of the commons introduced in chapter 1, drawing on Stavrides and De Angelis's idea of differing hierarchies of modes of production, the COPIM projects illustrate an organisational approach that favours more community-led, self-organised production over state and market forms. It therefore tips the scale towards a more commons-based mode of production and tones down the excesses of profit-seeking models.

It is also worth noting that COPIM is partly funded by UKRI, the national funding body of the UK, and so the state does play a part in the hierarchy between the market, state, and commons within OA publishing. Here, the funding arises out of UKRI's commitment to the open agenda, which they have nurtured through policies similar to those analysed in chapter 2. They also support infrastructure such as Octopus—the scientific platform for sharing all outcomes of the scientific process—and grassroots community approaches to openness such as the UK Reproducibility Network. Furthermore, in a similar vein, Latin

America has had a robust state-funded infrastructural ecosystem for OA publishing since the mid-1990s that continues to flourish today in the form of SciELO, Redalyc, AmeliCA, and others.[43] These projects represent a decentralised, noncommercial approach to publishing in journals and repositories, one that is highly successful and embedded in many countries in Latin America. Through these approaches we can see how the state may intervene to nurture forms of OA publishing that do not rely on policy mandates that force researcher behavioural change but may instead undermine the need to sustain and scale operations through commercial means. This is perhaps why many commercial organisations in the Global North see noncommercial forms of publishing to be a threat to pre-existing neoliberal understandings of market-led innovation.

For example, in a report produced by researchers at MIT entitled *Access to Science and Scholarship: Key Questions about the Future of Research Publishing*, the authors write:

> Diamond OA has worked on a larger scale in some regions, including South and Central America where national funders have built cooperative models such as SciELO. These large-scale, multimillion-dollar models have promise, but may be easier to build in areas that do not have established publishing infrastructure and expectations already in place. One question about this model concerns innovation: in a cooperative model with no competing journal publishers, there may be less incentive to invest in improvements. Many of the new tools valued by research funders and researchers (e.g. persistent identifiers, and paper mill and image manipulation detection tools) have been instigated by large publishers. If

> competition is removed or reduced, how will that impact the drive towards ongoing improvements in publishing infrastructure, in service to the research ecosystem, and how will those technological advances be funded?[44]

This passage indicates the kind of neocolonial responses that non-market-led approaches to publishing receive from Anglo-American contexts. For many advocates of commercial publishing, it is unimaginable that cooperative publishing projects, or those that do not rely on traditional notions of commercial sustainability, will be able to meet the "expectations" of an industry driven by profit and competition. For the authors of the report quoted above, innovation is something that arises out of market interactions, not from people working together to solve a problem or nurture new cultures of knowledge production. The only possible way for new tools to be developed, journals to be published, and infrastructure to be sustained is by commercial logic, even though it is clearly this commercial logic that besets publishing through consolidation, knowledge enclosures, and other forms of market imposition that lead to homogeneity. For Chan et al., this kind of thinking "feeds into the growing trend of nationalism and regionalism, with European nations and the EU willing to make deals with multinational publishers to secure their presence in research outputs."[45] At most, Global South countries are treated as beneficiaries of these outputs, rather than producers of knowledge in their own right.

Scaling small, and the related practices found in South-South publishing collaborations, can respond to this neoliberal imagination by offering a different approach to innovation, one based on collaboration, experimentation, and sociality. For Rebekka

Kiesewetter, these experiments imply "the performance of epistemic diversity, difference, and plurality within knowledge production in a way that caters to diverse situated knowledges, epistemologies, research cultures, and needs."[46] It is exactly this kind of epistemic diversity and bibliodiversity that commercial forms of knowledge production preclude, and these are the results that alternative approaches to scale and alliance-building might help encourage.

Yet this strategy of change requires actors to engage with institutions rather than withdraw from them. Such a strategy of continuous engagement is advocated by the political theorist Chantal Mouffe as an avenue of affective political engagement through artistic and cultural methods rather than more traditionally recognisable political means. To this end, Mouffe advocates a series of "counter-hegemonic interventions whose objective is to disrupt the smooth image that corporate capitalism tries to spread."[47] Scholar-led publishing disrupts the smooth image of corporate publishing by its very existence, revealing not only the extractive nature of the publishing industry but redirecting this extracted labour away from commercial to community-based forms. Scaling small therefore represents a counter-hegemonic challenge to the neoliberal institutional form, not as a replacement to it but as an illustration of the affective potential of alternative approaches. Scholar-led OA presses weave themselves together across different localities and geographies, while attracting others to do the same.

Scaling small therefore complicates the idea of openness or reveals its limits for a project so grounded in intentional, careful collaborations. The infrastructural projects being described here are difficult to sustain and develop, requiring significant effort to cultivate. We might think of these cultivations, decisions, and experiments as closures: they are the things that give meaning to the "open" in open access. So rather than leaving everything to the structurelessness of market-centric openness, through these different collaborations we learn how to deal with the fact that things like governance, careful publishing, and labour-intensive processes do not scale well according to economic logic. The infrastructural practices of scholar-led publishers require us to learn how to cultivate good closures in material-discursive decision-making.[48] Closures are the ways we take responsibility for our decision-making, the alliances we make, and the strategies we adopt. For Janneke Adema, these decisions represent a process of "continual critique":

> In our ongoing affirmative politics and practices of the open, we have to make decisions and thus close down the open; however, we can start to think more responsibly and ethically about the closures we enact and enable in our communication practices and through our systems of knowledge production: for instance, by focusing on creating difference as part of the decisions (which are also incisions or enactments of closure) we make, and by promoting otherness, variety, and processual becoming.[49]

The commons I am working towards, then, seeks to weave a path between openness and closure in order to create space for difference and sustain it. My argument is that the way to do this is through sociality—by experimenting with the various ways people get together, and providing infrastructural support for them to do so at different scales. This can be achieved through informal collaboration and mutual reliance or more formalised relationships between researchers, libraries, and other actors in the scholarly communication system. In each case, the social processes that go into the creation of the finished publication are just as important as the publication itself. It is only through process that we undermine commercial modes of production, not just providing free access to the end product.

Too much of the debate around OA publishing has focused on outputs, so my understanding of the commons attempts to reintroduce process into the meaning of OA. Conceived in this way, the design of infrastructures looks quite different, depending on whether you are merely facilitating free access to publications or foregrounding the messy social processes that lead to the creation of these outputs. Both are important, but too much of the debate around OA publishing focuses on the business models needed to freely disseminate research, and not the processes needed to disrupt the idea of business models altogether. This idea returns us to the formulation of the commons by Lauren Berlant discussed above, who argues that it is not about designing infrastructures to fit predefined understandings of collectivity, but about designing multiple infrastructural interventions to facilitate experiments in collectivity. From this perspective, the Radical Open Access Collective and other experiments in scaling small are designed to imagine and enact the infrastructural possibilities that allow us to learn to "live with messed up yet shared and ongoing infrastructures of experience."[50]

Conclusion

Beyond Open Access?

This book has attempted to make sense of the ongoing transition to OA publishing and what it means for more progressive approaches to publishing that do not rely on marketisation. Throughout the book I have explored a variety of OA publishing projects—including OA policies and scholar-led approaches—and how they conform to various understandings of "the commons." Although my argument is programmatic, I am less interested in how to make as many publications as possible openly accessible, and more concerned with the real consequences of the rise in commercial forms of OA and the possibilities of using this transition to push back against the extractive and revenue-generating nature of commercial publishing. In doing this, I have sought to understand an idea of the commons that foregrounds the transformative potential of the social processes that go into creating freely accessible publications and technical infrastructures.

To reiterate my argument in chapter 1, the commons requires an appreciation of the resources in question, the community that uses and manages the resources, and the social relations that govern them. This tripartite idea complicates naive liberal understandings of OA publishing that call it a commons simply because the publications are freely available to all, regardless of the ways they are produced and governed. This is to say that a progressive understanding of the commons treats the social processes as a mode of production that is distinct from market- and state-driven modes, though equally implicated in each. So rather than seeing it as an idealised separate, harmonious space, I have tried to conceive of the commons as elevating forms of production sustained by collectivity over those sustained by profitability and revenue generation. This process represents a messy and continuous struggle of carving out forms of collectivity within a world otherwise overrun by individualising market forces.

At this stage, is it worth asking, why open access? What is it about OA publishing that makes it useful for exploring alternative forms of commons-based publishing? Put simply, the academic publishing system is currently in flux and this creates space to nurture the commons. Taking inspiration again from Fred Moten and Stefano Harney, it is possible to "sneak into the university and steal what one can" to redirect these resources to better ethical and political ends.[1] If we understand the popularity of the push for OA publishing in purely material terms, there is a great deal of funding freed up for open access experimentation. Institutional publishers, policy interventions, and funding calls all open up space to do this. OA is the pet project of governments and funders across the world, allowing communities to experiment with alternative forms of publishing as long as the outputs are freely accessible to all.

Furthermore, while commercial publishing is not unique in its extraction of free labour for profit, it is impossible to ignore that the profit margins of commercial publishers are sustained largely by the free labour of authors, editors, reviewers, and copyeditors (among others). Academics, for the most part, are not remunerated directly for this labour, which is an increasing burden as more research is published, and it can be put to better ends through alternative publishing efforts. The OA debate is a constant reminder of the free work we give publishers, and it offers an opportunity to support commons-based efforts by withdrawing and redirecting our efforts. This is what we hope to achieve with the Radical Open Access Collective: a space to show academics that there is a much better place to put their labour through DIY forms of publishing.

This does not mean that I think OA—i.e., public access to research—is not valuable, but more that it is the bare minimum that new, ethical systems of publishing should be facilitating. Or rather, it is not enough for policymakers to congratulate themselves on all the open access publications they have facilitated if all the profits of these publications go straight into shareholders' pockets. OA publishing simply recreates all the problems associated with commercial subscription publishing if it does not address the marketised mode of production that is purely extractive and prevents the exploration of the commons that I theorise here. Publishing requires the kinds of care and human expertise that commercial models cannot support because they are in their very nature designed to minimise human expense and extract the surplus. While OA offers the chance to fund publishing in ways that go beyond market interaction, the dominant forms of OA make commercialisation worse.

Indeed, the rise of "transformative agreements" for OA as a replacement to the traditional subscription model makes technological automation and high-volume publishing the most attractive option for commercial publishers looking to increase their revenue. These agreements charge universities one price to read a publisher's content and to publish OA too, without additional fees (which is why they are often referred to as "read and publish" deals). The agreements therefore reward presses that can publish as many articles as possible, so that they will appear valuable to universities seeking to support the sites where their academics publish.[2] Yet the upshot of this business model is that publishers attempt to funnel as many publications through their platforms as they can, often with little human oversight or editorial care. This has led to a rise in paper mills, fraudulent articles characterised by data manipulation, and citation rings of researchers legitimising fraudulent research by citing each other favourably, all based on publishers wanting to publish more articles without providing the labour to do so properly. The publisher Wiley had to shut down one of the OA imprints it acquired, Hindawi, and retract thousands of articles due to these problems, and they are far from unique.[3] The volume-driven models of OA created by the publishing industry strip publishing down to a bare service, undermining the editorial communities that shape the work and seeking to automate everything to the greatest extent possible.

One currently popular response to the situation of profiteering through OA is the current push in the UK and Europe for policies based on "rights retention" and secondary publishing rights, which allow authors to retain the rights to distribute their work without paying article-processing charges. These policies allow authors to self-archive their accepted manuscripts by either granting such rights in legislation, or requiring research to retain the rights to self-archive the paper as a condition of publication.[4] Rights retention is increasingly common in Europe in response to the extractive nature of transformative agreements and the one-sided nature of journal negotiations in which publishers are in a much better bargaining position. Rights retention policies are said to "weaken publishers' negotiation positions" by making accepted articles available in repositories (green OA).[5] This means they are less able to rely on monopolistic control of the version of record and are therefore forced to negotiate a fairer price for libraries.

Although rights retention policies are a good way to make research outputs freely available, it is wishful thinking to expect them to have any impact on the market at large and the means of production that I refer to above. This wishful thinking represents an extension of the idea (discussed in chapter 1) that a fairer market will be created by academics making price-sensitive decisions about where to publish. In each case, the logic is based on the notion that there can be a fair, competitive market for scholarly publishing if only the conditions are correct. However, the intense concentration of the industry, coupled with the fact that researchers are required to publish in certain places for career reasons, will ensure that commercial power remains in the hands of a small number of for-profit publishers. Universities are trapped in a cycle of marketisation, beset by administrators who are unable—and certainly unwilling—to entertain the idea that marketisation has failed. Rights retention clearly does not begin to address this political situation.

Perhaps, instead, it is worth viewing open access, following Thomas Hervé Mboa Nkoudou, as a "pharmakon," which in Derrida's usage refers to something that is both a poison and a cure.[6] Mboa Nkoudou emphasises the "epistemic alienation" of African research by OA publishing that reinforces the use of research from "the center of the world-system, while consolidating Eurocentric thought as the global theoretical reference or normative model, to the detriment of local epistemologies."[7] By the same token, the increasing success of "open access" as a "movement" only increases the commercial viability of academic publishing, which merely perpetuates the original problems of marketisation. In each case, the cure of free access to knowledge is also its poison. Yet despite this, Mboa Nkoudou is not willing to "abandon" OA publishing, and instead advocates redesigning it as a tool of cognitive justice through a decolonized approach to scholarly communication. While I am wholly in favour of decolonising scholarly communication, I am also sceptical that OA is a helpful frame for such a practice; it may be simply that the OA "movement" itself has now run its course.

In many ways, this book has been about how we can think through, and thus in some ways leave behind or at least decentre, OA publishing in favour of a radical approach to the commons that deals with how knowledge is produced rather than simply how it is disseminated. The commons frame resonates with many issues beyond publishing and requires responses based on much more than whether a publication is open or closed. Yet I am hesitant to broaden out from OA publishing too much, not least because of the dangers of grand-solution-based arguments for political change that end up homogenising the situations they are describing and that they are attempting to intervene in. Politics is not rolling out a grand, predetermined plan, but rather a series of critical struggles with actors who share a common horizon. The importance of smallness and situatedness cannot be overstated here.

Nevertheless, the commons is helpful in its appreciation of community governance: the idea that groups of people can come together to build and share resources and maintain them in the long run. This idea of community governance offers a productive route to a possible future strategy for forms of publishing that are not simply about open access to resources but focus more on cultures of knowledge production within and outside the traditional university space. This returns us to the idea that, above all, the commons is about sociality, care, horizontality, and embedding these dynamics in the institutions we create. By way of a conclusion that looks forward to future possibilities, the following sections detail a series of avenues for exploration into governing the scholarly commons.

Governing the Scholarly Commons

Many of the projects and interventions I have discussed in this book represent a mode of publishing governed by communities rather than profit-seeking organisations. The scholar-led publishing ecosystem is a publishing model managed by academics, while the philosophy of scaling small could facilitate collaboration among libraries, university presses, technology providers, and others involved in scholarly communication. These projects represent a more collective approach to governance and the decentring of market imperatives as the main form of accountability. With this turn towards accountability comes the need to reassess standard governance structures and processes and to make them more democratic and intentional. In general, scholarly communication and publishing projects suffer from weak or underdeveloped governance processes.[8] This is not just the case for for-profit models produced by large commercial presses—it affects start-ups, nonprofits, and smaller community projects too. Good governance requires coordination and effort, entailing the devolution of power to a broader range of stakeholders and not just those with an immediate connection to the project. Yet, too often, founders and organisers of all kinds of projects either see governance procedures as a lower priority than sustainability and day-to-day management or they are reluctant to cede power to others in the name of governance.

In any case, community governance is one of the key requirements for more commons-based systems of publishing, and in many other areas of higher education. It is therefore an area that needs much more experimentation. Governance is of particular importance in the struggle over user data and the extent to which it may be owned by corporations and processed by sophisticated predictive algorithms.[9] Users need control over their data—or at least a say in how it is used—and governance structures can facilitate this. These governance issues are increasingly significant to academic publishing, especially in the context of the "datafied" strategies of large commercial publishers aimed at amassing and processing as much data as possible. Put simply, research communities need control over the infrastructures and technologies they use, and this is where formalised governance procedures and structures can help.

For Elinor Ostrom, good governance is "adaptive" in how it responds to the evolution of community rules and norms over time. Successful adaptive governance, for Ostrom, depends on a number of factors, including "providing information, dealing with conflict, inducing rule compliance, providing infrastructure, and being prepared for change."[10] However, these requirements may be met in a "wide diversity" of ways; there is no blueprint for good community governance, not least because all communities are different and constantly changing. Another way to say this is that governance is situated to the community in question: it looks quite different whether you are a distributed online community working on open-source software development or a rural community managing their local reservoir, for example. Both approaches necessitate rules for their community-led operations, but these rules will obviously be very different. The local focus of governance also means it does not scale well with a larger number of community members or greater geographical complexity, which is why smaller communities can more easily govern their work than larger ones. This means that direct democratic forms of governance are more difficult in large, multi-user communities.

While "scaling small" is an approach to infrastructural design and governance that begins from the idea that locality is the best way to preserve diversity in the broader publishing ecosystem, it is also important to appreciate that scholarly communication is shaped by multinational corporations and infused with capitalist logic. Strategies to reorient publishing away from marketisation need to adopt a similar approach to smallness in order to intervene in the market at the appropriate scale. This means avoiding ineffective tactics such as boycotts or other approaches to ethical consumerism, much like the now-dormant "Cost of Knowledge" boycott, which asked signatories to not review or author papers for Elsevier due to its commercial practices and opposition to open access.[11] These approaches are ineffective at instigating political change because of their indiscriminate nature and overall lack of strategy; this is evidenced by the fact that 38 percent of the signatories of the Cost of Knowledge boycott had abandoned their commitment within four years of signing it.[12] Boycotts are not good governance, because they are based on individual decision-making rather than well-organised collective action: researchers have no real power as consumers in the publishing market.

Perhaps it is also the often-apolitical nature of the demand for more OA that limits the vision of those wishing to change publishing for the better. Demands for OA can easily be met by commercial publishers charging extortionate fees for OA. Elsevier is now one of the world's largest open access publishers and has managed to subsume the calls for greater OA into its highly successful business model. Boycotts and other calls for change in publishing are often based on whether the organisation is promoting open access, when the problem is exactly the fact that OA is being co-opted by commercial actors. This co-optation is another reason to leave behind the language of open vs. closed and instead focus on undermining market imperatives through governance interventions, i.e., the things we can control.

For De Angelis and Stavrides, the practice of commoning is a useful touchstone here. Drawing on Marx's understanding of the factory as a space of both capitalist exploitation *and* the social cooperation of labour, they argue that social relations within workplaces make commoning more possible, despite being exploited by capital. For example, they write, in the factory "If I need a tool, I ask you to pass me one. If I need a piece of information, I do not have to pay a copyright."[13] Despite its hierarchies and the whims of the market, the factory itself reflects labour as a social process, or what De Angelis and Stavrides term "distorted commoning," distorted because it is extracted by capitalism as an input in the production process and allows it to thrive. The commoning in the workplace also offers opportunities for worker self-organisation, such as union activity and other forms of collective action.

In a similar vein, commercial publishing houses are able to exploit the practices of commoning undertaken by editorial boards in the service of managing their journals. Publishers do this by relying on the social glue that holds the journal together and ensures that journal content is well edited, reviewed, and published in a timely manner. The academic work of editing a journal is mostly undertaken for free by groups of people working together to produce knowledge without the aim of commercial gain, even though their work is ultimately extracted for revenue by the publisher. Under commercial models of open access, the relationship between publisher and editorial community is increasingly strained as publishers pressure editors to accept more articles that lead to more APCs. But despite this pressure, or maybe because of it, the editorial ownership of a journal is a powerful tool for governing scholarly publishing. Editorial boards are simultaneously inside and outside the publishing market, able to push back on certain publisher policies and to withdraw their labour altogether. They have an underappreciated potential for governing the scholarly commons through collective action.

Editorial Board Governance

There has been a recent upsurge of editorial board resignations in response to publisher policies and business models, including from the *Journal of Biogeography*, *Design Studies*, *Publications*, *NeuroImage*, and *Critical Public Health*. Many editors cite publisher restrictions on editorial control as the reason to leave, including over editorial leadership, open access fees, and pressure to lower peer review standards to accept more articles.[14] For example, in their resignation letter, the former editors of *Critical Public Health* write:

> The new contract and amendment issued to the editors make clear the limited role the publisher sees for the editorial team and board. In reiterating the rights of the publisher to determine the funding model and volume of articles that will be published, we believe Taylor & Francis have significantly eroded our ability to set strategic direction. The editorial team's ability to manage a collegial and bespoke response to authors and reviewers has also been systematically undermined by changes (typically without any consultation) to the submission platform, information about the journal, and requirements for manuscripts, and outsourcing key functions such as pre-production. The only model offered for ensuring authors can publish open access has been Article Processing Charges (APCs), currently £2700 per research article: an unsustainable cost for research funders and university libraries in high income countries, and an impossible cost for many in less advantaged countries; occasional subsidies do not constitute a viable solution to the much deeper issues of inequity embedded within the profit orientation.[15]

This passage represents a rich and thorough assessment of the direction of commercial publishing and the influence of commercial decision-making on editorial control over the publishing process. The editors emphasise the problem of publishers claiming the sole power to set policy without input from editorial communities. In doing so, they draw attention to the lack of control that academic researchers have over the future of publishing.

Paradoxically, the current lack of governance or oversight of publishing policies illustrates the opportunity that editorial board governance holds for gaining more accountability over scholarly communication. Editorial board resignations normalise returning control to research communities and downplaying commerciality as the dominant ordering logic. While we should not overemphasise their promise to transform publishing, resignations can be considered a form of scaling small that may become more important as more researchers participate and negotiate better terms for their journals. Collective action by editorial boards could be facilitated through union structures or organisations like the Radical Open Access Collective. These approaches would provide resources on how to interact as an editorial board and present a unified front for negotiations, allowing editors from across publishers and disciplines to interact and have their demands met.

Many of the editorial boards who resign go on to launch new journals with other presses or to self-publish their work entirely as scholar-led publishers. For example, the editors of the Elsevier journal *Lingua* resigned en masse in protest of the high price of Elsevier's open access options.[16] The editors launched the diamond open access journal *Glossa* with the Open Library of Humanities, while referring to the original journal as "Zombie Lingua" to discourage others from submitting.[17] The original journal still exists under the leadership of a new editorial board, although its reputation remains tarnished. Similarly, the editors of the Elsevier journal *NeuroImage* resigned over the "greed" of Elsevier and its "unethical" OA publishing charges that bear "no relation to the costs involved."[18] They launched *Imaging Neuroscience* with MIT Press, a fully OA journal that has an article-processing charge roughly half that of Elsevier's.

Editorial board resignations often reflect a vision of publishing shaped by marketisation that assumes commerciality is inescapable. The *Imaging Neuroscience* editors do not reject the article-processing charge model entirely, despite its inherently inequitable nature, and instead opt for a charge of $1600 in their new journal. Similarly, the resignation statement of the *Journal of Biogeography* editors contains a reference to the editors' success in increasing submissions and increasing the journal's impact factor, both arbitrary metrics that reflect the business of publishing rather than the journal's scientific merit.[19] It is important, therefore, that editorial board governance not focus on incrementally better forms of OA, but on good, ethical forms of publishing that are well supported and intentionally constructed by research communities. The landscape of scholar-led publishing collectives discussed in the previous chapter has hegemonic potential to influence and encourage academic governance in publishing. Importantly, the strategy of increasing governance of publishing is less about OA and more about designing the structures that allow research communities to control scholarly communication collectively. This does not mean, unlike with scholar-led publishing, that academics manage the entire process of publishing, but rather that accountability and direction rest with scholarly communities instead of shareholders and the market at large.

Learned Societies

Academic societies are frequently cited as a point of resistance in the ongoing transition to OA publishing. Reliant on library budgets to sustain their activities through increasingly inflated journal subscription prices, many societies have written extensively in opposition to the movement for making knowledge freely available, considering this move a threat to their own existence.[20] While learned societies cannot be painted with a broad brush, many do indeed maintain reserves of millions of dollars and pay their senior staff sizeable salaries, despite being "nonprofit" in the sense that they cannot return revenue to shareholders. They are strongly reliant on the commercial model of publishing that I seek to resist here.

It is tempting to see learned societies as unnecessary, too commercially minded, something that academia can eradicate without consequence. This would be a mistake. Increasing attacks on higher education, and on humanities disciplines specifically, reveal a need for collective action and self-organisation in the service of solidarity and defending the value of academic research. Societies of varying sizes and disciplinary scopes can offer this collectivity outside the walls of the traditional university, provided they are equitably and democratically governed by their membership. Currently, the society form is more likely to be hierarchical and conservative, distributing resources in the form of travel grants and bursaries to early-career researchers through opaque processes based on traditional notions of university careers that only exist for a minority of fortunate researchers.

A great deal of work has gone into trying to make OA publishing work for learned societies. cOAlition S has funded work to design models to allow societies to convert to open access and still maintain their revenue, while many others are using the Subscribe to Open approach, which makes a journal open access when enough libraries subscribe.[21] Commercial publishers are positioning themselves as service providers for learned societies, such as through Wiley's "partner services" model, which offers a range of tools to allow societies to manage their own publishing process, rather than doing it in collaboration with a publisher and sharing the revenue. Irrespective of the size of the learned society and the debate around open access, society revenues will continue to decrease as library budgets further constrict. This is a long-standing problem that has been entangled, often incorrectly, with the move to open access under the assumption that it is the cause of learned societies' financial woes. The societies who were previously beneficiaries of the marketisation of publishing are now finding themselves victims of it.

This problem presents an opportunity to reform societies through nurturing grassroots cultures of academic collectivity. Despite often being hierarchical, societies have the potential to bring together academics in interesting and radical ways, working across institutions, geographies, and subdisciplines. They therefore represent an exciting area for nurturing cultures of knowledge production outside the marketised university. But instead of creating a predefined notion of the academic society, we might think of this work as the exploration of new academic *socialities*—organisational forms that facilitate horizontal ways of working, resource distribution, and mutual reliance. This approach is already being promoted through organisations such as Neuromatch, a globally distributed network of neuroscience researchers focusing on sharing teaching materials, open publishing, and community building and mentorship.[22] Neuromatch hosts a conference and an open-source social media network on the Mastodon platform, and is designing a platform for self-publishing neuroscience research. It is a self-governed organisation for knowledge production and communication, a break from the top-down societies that are more commonplace. Many more experimental organisations of this kind are necessary to explore a future for noncommercial, horizontally governed academic societies.

Rather than looking for the best ways to financially sustain learned societies in a post-open access world, I suggest that the work needed is to design structures for democratic self-governance of societies. Working in the service of a loosely shared horizon of commons-based knowledge production, societies could be designed and reformed in ways that facilitate self-organisation and collaboration, particularly against capitalistic knowledge practices and the marketisation of higher education. This experimentation could be achieved through a series of governance processes designed by and for societies of different sizes and scopes, learning from cooperatives and commons organisations across different sectors.

Research Assessment Reform

A final governance intervention I want to explore against marketisation relates to the current push in higher education for research assessment reform, particularly reforms designed to value a multitude of open research practices and scholarly contributions. This push is often motivated by the laudable aim of allowing researchers to publish in the ways they choose, not in the ways that hiring committees and journal brands dictate. Organisations such as the Declaration on Research Assessment (DORA) and the Coalition for Advancing Research Assessment seek to eradicate the inappropriate metrics used to identify research quality, particularly the H-Index and the Journal Impact Factor, and replace them with a more appropriate plurality of qualitative and quantitative measures.

For example, the recent European agreement on reforming research assessment makes recommendations to recognise those "diverse outputs, practices and activities that maximise the quality and impact of research."[23] The implication is that good research is being done, but that it is not possible to learn this from current approaches to research assessment that prioritise novel or fashionable research over rigorous scholarship. This issue has a particular bearing on hiring processes that reward prestigious publications, usually owned by large commercial publishers, partly because such measures are an easy stand-in for research quality for assessors faced with hundreds of applications for jobs and grants. In its place, the declaration argues for the centrality of peer review supported by "responsible use of quantitative indicators."

In place of traditional metricised approaches to assessment, many advocates of assessment reform propose alternative, qualitative processes for judging researchers, such as the narrative CV. According to a report by DORA, these CVs present a "concise, but structured way for authors to provide qualitative evidence for a broad array of outputs and outcomes from research" that can be assessed "more evenly across a pool of applicants."[24] Narrative CVs allow researchers to contextualise their contributions and provide a more holistic picture of the work they have done. They therefore move away from lists of publications and grant awards and allow researchers to describe their work in their own words, which may help researchers who are not following a traditional academic career path.

While narrative CVs are by no means the only reform being proposed to research assessment, they are indicative of the political corner into which many reformers have backed themselves that makes proposing radical reforms impossible. Narrative CVs may allow researchers to present a fuller picture of their work, but they also entail more work on the part of applicants and assessors to move away from standardised CVs and adequately review this non-standardised format. Tanita Casci argues that this may lead to "disadvantages for non-native speakers, minoritized groups, and those without support from the institution in completing the CV template."[25] Like many of the problems in the university, research assessment reform is a problem of defunding higher education that better ways of assessing researchers will not address. Assessment reform therefore assumes that tinkering with hiring structures will lead to fairer ways of evaluating research, when the problems are both political and systemic and therefore require radical collective organisation.

Viewed instead through a lens of governance, it is clear to see how research assessment reform is a labour issue rather than a simple epistemological one. It is about the increasingly competitive material conditions that we in the university labour under, the precarious conditions under which we work, and the fact that these labour issues have negative epistemological outcomes that lead to a range of poor research behaviours. Top-down reforms to research assessment are necessarily problematic because they do not expand governance to the researchers at the bleeding edge of precarity or work towards greater democratisation of the university. Instead, they presuppose that there is a correct way to reward those doing the "best" work, and that identifying the best work is even possible. Rarely is the idea of eradicating researcher assessment itself entertained; instead, a variety of experiments are proposed to sort and assess people without tackling the underlying labour conditions that lead to such brutal research cultures.

Like greater governance by editorial boards and within learned societies, governance over the university can help introduce care into university assessment processes and downplay marketisation. Research assessment reform should be seen as more about governance than about getting assessment procedures correct, i.e., it should be about getting structures in place so that people in the university can decide these issues collectively. How do we reduce hierarchies within academic departments, labs, and universities to better distribute resources based on nurturing equitable cultures of research, not on rewarding the "best" individuals? The answer to this question reveals the value of thinking in terms of collectivity and the commons in order to democratise different spaces in the university.

The push to better recognise the contributions of all people involved in the research process is another good way to do this. Currently, academic systems of credit sort people into those who are authors and those who are not, often excluding people in "support" roles such as librarians, technicians, and data stewards who may make substantial contributions to research. Teperek et al. have argued for abandoning the distinction between academic and professional service roles, primarily because this distinction "discourages a culture of collaboration and appreciation of a diversity of roles and contributions."[26] I would go further and argue that traditional roles do not make sense without those in so-called support positions. Their labour contributes to each research article and should be credited as such, simply because papers are the way scholarly labour is recognised. Again, not to belabour the point too much, this is a question of expanding the definition of who gets to govern the structures of knowledge production and who gets to count as an "author."

Projects such as HuMetricsHSS take a different approach, seeking to broaden the kinds of practices and processes that can be measured, to promote a "values-enacted scholarship."[27] The project team puts forward a well-considered framework based on values of equity, openness, collegiality, soundness, and community, aiming to instantiate these values as part of researcher assessment processes such as the tenure process in the United States.[28] Crucially, the project does not shy away from the fact that these values should be "locally negotiated" rather than introduced in a top-down or indiscriminate fashion. This is not a naive project to work out how to rank researchers according to new values; it is instead an argument for researcher-governed processes that reflect and extend the values we hold dear within the university.

The governance issues discussed here are not so much about open access, but about taking power from the market and redistributing it equitably across higher education. Or rather, these issues point to avenues of exploration for commons-based governance beyond those I have explored relating to OA publishing. I hope I have shown practical ways to approach this task, keeping in mind that it is not a question of open vs. closed, but of how to increase self-organisation within and across universities and publishing projects, particularly by those currently excluded from this governance. Issues of publishing, learned societies, and research assessment are also rarely a significant concern of academic unions (at least, as I am framing them), but could be added to their agendas as part of the struggle for a more emancipatory culture of higher education worldwide. The rise of collective action in response to labour conditions in universities is one of the more promising avenues of struggle and shares common cause with many of the issues discussed in this book.[29] In making this common cause, a more progressive approach to governance might be possible within higher education.

Commons Policy Futures

Invoking my earlier discussion of Lauren Berlant, I am at pains to stress that we must be careful to not ask too much of the commons and self-governance. Berlant uses the idea of the commons to explore the possibilities of infrastructural experimentation for new forms of sociality, rather than designing infrastructures in terms of a predefined idea of what a "common" society might look like. This is why no blueprint is possible for the commons. We can only hope to instigate and encourage new and better forms of horizontal governance so that (we) the commoners can experiment and decide for ourselves, rather than being imposed on by multinational corporations governed by profit-seeking and other commercial imperatives. If we take as our goal the replacement of all commercial publishing practices with those grounded in the commons, we will be swallowed up by the market and its drive for homogeneity, economies of scale, and totalisation. Yet if we take a smaller approach of experimentation and intervention—one that purposefully eschews homogeneity and promotes locality and community—it is possible to find pockets of radical activity that can be sustained with care and conviviality in an otherwise commercial environment. I hope to have shown a wide variety of projects throughout this book that display this care and conviviality, along with the dangers of mandating forms of publishing that do not.

So if open access publishing is to have a future, rather than just being subsumed into the publishing industry through "transformative" agreements, it will need to make space for these bibliodiverse and careful forms of publishing and not foreclose their possible futures. Indeed, for Gary Hall, an ethical approach to OA is one that requires us to continually leave this question undecided:

> We cannot therefore state that the manner in which open access enables us to keep questions of ethics, politics, cultural studies, disciplinarity, and the university open is political always and forever. This decision is one we constantly need to (re)take anew: both because we can never be sure that our previous decisions were the correct, or the best, or at any rate the least worst ones we could have taken; and because any such open-access archive will keep on being confronted with texts that are different in both form and content, and thus in effect new potential parasites, viruses, and unwelcome guests.[30]

For Hall, openness means openness to indeterminacy and change, meaning that our infrastructures and practices of scholarly publishing (and the university) should be changeable too. Just as OA publishing will keep being confronted with different texts, so too will it be driven by different policymakers and political agendas, all of which require engagement with—rather than withdrawal from—these institutions that shape our lives. This text is my own small attempt to engage with such actors and spheres.

OA policy may be especially shaped by changing international tensions between national superpowers. In this light, one of the chief architects of Plan S suggested a "geo-walling" approach to scholarly material that makes research openly accessible only to those of certain localities, in order to exclude those who gain a competitive advantage from open access without reciprocating.[31] While there is nothing new about scientific nationalism—science policy has always been conducted according to dominant countries' political agendas—the waning of the liberal consensus does have implications for liberal understandings of scientific "openness" and what open access might look like. Is the neoliberal rationality of fixing the publishing market through OA enough to trump the rise of governments that want to legislate only in their citizens' narrowly defined interests?

Similarly, EU governments are showing an ambition to rein in the extractive practices of social media companies, AI organisations, and data brokers, returning control to end users of these technologies and preventing harm—"democracy beginning to take back the void," as Shoshana Zuboff describes it.[32] While I am less sanguine about the EU's regulatory ability, the shift towards data ownership and regulation does open up avenues for community governance, certainly coupled with its proposed agenda to foreground "nonprofit" publishers within open access policymaking.[33] In each case, the commons acts as a helpful counterpoint to liberal ideas of openness, which are being left behind in any meaningful sense. Rather than arguing for more open data or open-source platforms, to counter the threat of closed technologies, these issues are better framed in terms of community governance and the necessity for users to have a say in the technologies they use and are used by—especially for commercial purposes. For Jeff Pooley, the urgency of these issues requires a "full-fledged campaign, leveraging activism and legislative pressure, to challenge the commercial publishers' extractive agenda," although what this would look like in practice is difficult to tell.[34]

The commons as the self-organisation of labour is a much more helpful touchstone here than OA publishing or openness. The commons promotes community governance, a local focus, and the need to ensure proper boundaries that may not be crossed by commercial organisations, while also downplaying the market as the gold standard of production. This is one of the key reasons to leave OA publishing—and openness—behind and instead argue for an agenda that promotes good closures and community responsibility. A huge amount of work needs to be done on the practical ways communities may govern the technologies they use and the frameworks they can build to govern them, but this work is much more productive than working out the best ways to make academic research freely available.

You might feel that this chapter has moved quite far from OA publishing, and this is exactly the point I am making. OA is a case study for the ideas I am discussing and the forms of organisation that can lead to good, ethical cultures of commoning. The OA projects I discuss here offer the chance to see what community governance looks like within a higher education setting and how it can be "scaled small" in the furtherance of a common(s) horizon. Although this process will entail a series of continuous struggles, it is certainly something worth struggling for.

Notes

Introduction

1. BOAI, "Budapest Open Access Initiative," 2002, http://www.budapestopenaccessinitiative.org/read

2. BOAI.

3. Heather Piwowar, Jason Priem, and Richard Orr, "The Future of OA: A Large-Scale Analysis Projecting Open Access Publication and Readership," preprint (Scientific Communication and Education, October 9, 2019), https://doi.org/10.1101/795310

4. Stuart Lawson, "Open Access Policy in the UK: From Neoliberalism to the Commons" (PhD diss., London, Birkbeck College, 2019), http://stuartlawson.org/wp-content/uploads/2018/08/2018-08-30-thesis-draft.pdf; Gareth Johnson, "Through Struggle and Indifference: The UK Academy's Engagement with the Open Intellectual Commons" (PhD diss., Nottingham Trent, 2017); Janneke Adema, "Knowledge Production Beyond The Book? Performing the Scholarly Monograph in Contemporary Digital Culture" (PhD diss., Coventry University, 2015).

5. Stevan Harnad, "For Whom the Gate Tolls? From Stevan Harnad," *American-Scientist-Open-Access-Forum*, 1998, http://users.ecs.soton.ac.uk/harnad/Hypermail/Amsci/0001.html

6. Samuel A. Moore, "A Genealogy of Open Access: Negotiations between Openness and Access to Research," *Revue Française Des Sci-*

ences de l'information et de La Communication, no. 11 (2017), https://doi.org/10.4000/rfsic.3220

7. Rick Anderson, "Open Access and Academic Freedom: Teasing Out Some Important Nuances," *Development and Change* 52, no. 6 (2021): 1503–12, https://doi.org/10.1111/dech.12636; Samuel A. Moore, "Open Access, Plan S and 'Radically Liberatory' Forms of Academic Freedom," *Development and Change* 52, no. 6 (January 29, 2021), https://doi.org/10.1111/dech.12640

8. Charlotte Hess and Elinor Ostrom, *Understanding Knowledge as a Commons: From Theory to Practice* (Cambridge, MA: MIT Press, 2007), 3, http://public.eblib.com/choice/publicfullrecord.aspx?p=3338502

9. George Caffentzis, "A Tale of Two Conferences: Globalization, the Crisis of Neoliberalism and Question of the Commons," *Centre for Global Justice*, 2004.

10. Elinor Ostrom, *Governing the Commons: The Evolution of Institutions for Collective Action*, The Political Economy of Institutions and Decisions (Cambridge, UK: Cambridge University Press, 2008).

11. Michael Hardt and Antonio Negri, *Commonwealth* (Cambridge, MA: Belknap Press of Harvard University Press, 2009); Silvia Federici, *Caliban and the Witch* (New York: Autonomedia, 2004).

12. Heather Morrison, "About Sustaining the Knowledge Commons/À Propos Des Savoirs Communs," Sustaining the Knowledge Commons/Soutenir les savoirs communs, June 23, 2014, https://sustainingknowledgecommons.org/about/

13. Jeroen Bosman et al., "The Scholarly Commons—Principles and Practices to Guide Research Communication" (Open Science Framework, 2017), https://osf.io/6c2xt/

14. Peter Suber, "Creating an Intellectual Commons through Open Access," in *Understanding Knowledge as a Commons: From Theory to Practice*, ed. Charlotte Hess and Elinor Ostrom (Cambridge, MA: MIT Press, 2007).

15. Kathleen Shearer, "Building a Global Knowledge Commons through Open Access and Open Science" (Positioning Asia in the Global Movement of Open Science, Kuala Lumpur, Malaysia, 2016), accessed October 25, 2019, https://www.coar-repositories.org/files/shearer-AsiaOA-Nov2016.pdf

16. Ernesto Laclau, *On Populist Reason* (London: Verso, 2005), 89.
17. Moore, "A Genealogy of Open Access."
18. Gary Hall, *Digitize This Book! The Politics of New Media, or Why We Need Open Access Now* (Minneapolis: University of Minnesota Press, 2008); John Willinsky, *The Access Principle: The Case for Open Access to Research and Scholarship* (Cambridge, MA: MIT Press, 2006); Martin Paul Eve, *Open Access and the Humanities: Contexts, Controversies and the Future* (Cambridge: Cambridge University Press, 2014); Peter Baldwin, *Athena Unbound: Why and How Scholarly Knowledge Should Be Free for All* (Cambridge, MA: MIT Press, 2023).
19. Baldwin, *Athena Unbound*, 35.
20. James Wilsdon et al., "The Metric Tide: Report of the Independent Review of the Role of Metrics in Research Assessment and Management," 2015, http://doi.org/10.13140/RG.2.1.4929.1363
21. Eve, *Open Access and the Humanities*, 45.
22. Vincent Larivière, Stefanie Haustein, and Philippe Mongeon, "The Oligopoly of Academic Publishers in the Digital Era," ed. Wolfgang Glanzel, *PLOS ONE* 10, no. 6 (June 10, 2015): e0127502, https://doi.org/10.1371/journal.pone.0127502
23. Stefanie Haustein et al., "Estimating Global Article Processing Charges Paid to Six Publishers for Open Access between 2019 and 2023" (arXiv, July 23, 2024), https://doi.org/10.48550/arXiv.2407.16551
24. Jeff Pooley, "Surveillance Publishing," *Journal of Electronic Publishing* 25, no. 1 (April 26, 2022), https://doi.org/10.3998/jep.1874; Alejandro Posada and George Chen, "Inequality in Knowledge Production: The Integration of Academic Infrastructure by Big Publishers," in *22nd International Conference on Electronic Publishing* (22nd International Conference on Electronic Publishing, OpenEdition Press, 2018), https://doi.org/10.4000/proceedings.elpub.2018.30
25. Pooley, "Surveillance Publishing."
26. Cameron Neylon et al., *Open Scholarship and the Need for Collective Action* (Knowledge Exchange, 2019), 51, http://repository.jisc.ac.uk/7542/2/Open_Scholarship_and_the_need_for_collective_action_Oct_2019.pdf
27. Theodore C. Bergstrom et al., "Evaluating Big Deal Journal Bun-

dles," *Proceedings of the National Academy of Sciences* 111, no. 26 (July 1, 2014): 9425–30, https://doi.org/10.1073/pnas.1403006111

28. Stephen Buranyi, "Is the Staggeringly Profitable Business of Scientific Publishing Bad for Science?" *The Guardian*, June 27, 2017, sec. Science, http://www.theguardian.com/science/2017/jun/27/profitable-business-scientific-publishing-bad-for-science

29. Fei Shu et al., "Is It Such a Big Deal? On the Cost of Journal Use in the Digital Era," *College & Research Libraries* 79, no. 6 (2018), Fig. 2, https://doi.org/10.5860/crl.79.6.785

30. Andrew Odlyzko, "The Economics of Electronic Journals," *First Monday* 2, no. 8 (August 4, 1997), https://doi.org/10.5210/fm.v2i8.542

31. Bo-Christer Björk, "Evolution of the Scholarly Mega-Journal, 2006–2017," *PeerJ* 6 (9 February 2018): e4357, https://doi.org/10.7717/peerj.4357; Walt Crawford, *Gold Open Access 2013–2018: Articles in Journals* (Livermore, CA: Cites & Insights Books, 2019), https://waltcrawford.name/goa4.pdf

32. OpenAPC, "OpenAPC—Open APC," OpenAPC, no date, https://treemaps.openapc.net/apcdata/openapc/publisher

33. Dan Pollock and Ann Michael, "News & Views: Market Sizing Update 2023," Delta Think, October 24, 2023, https://deltathink.com/news-views-market-sizing-update-2023/; Haustein et al., "Estimating Global Article Processing Charges."

34. Shaun Yon-Seng Khoo, "Article Processing Charge Hyperinflation and Price Insensitivity: An Open Access Sequel to the Serials Crisis," *LIBER Quarterly* 29, no. 1 (May 9, 2019): 1, https://doi.org/10.18352/lq.10280

35. Thomas Klebel and Tony Ross-Hellauer, "The APC-Barrier and Its Effect on Stratification in Open Access Publishing," *Quantitative Science Studies* 4, no. 1 (March 1, 2023): 22–43, https://doi.org/10.1162/qss_a_00245

36. Hugo Radice, "How We Got Here: UK Higher Education under Neoliberalism," *ACME: An International Journal for Critical Geographies* 12, no. 2 (2013): 407–18.

37. Michel Foucault, *The Birth of Biopolitics: Lectures at the Collège de France, 1978–79*, trans. Michel Senellart (Basingstoke: Palgrave Macmillan, 2008), 226.

38. Sarah Lamdan, *Data Cartels: The Companies That Control and Monopolize Our Information* (Stanford, CA: Stanford University Press, 2023).

39. Wendy Brown, *Undoing the Demos: Neoliberalism's Stealth Revolution* (New York: Zone Books, 2015), 10.

40. Aileen Fyfe et al., "Untangling Academic Publishing: A History of the Relationship between Commercial Interests, Academic Prestige and the Circulation of Research," 2017, https://research-repository.st-andrews.ac.uk/bitstream/handle/10023/10884/Fyfe_etal_UntanglingAcPub_CC.pdf?sequence=1

41. Buranyi, "Is the Staggeringly Profitable Business of Scientific Publishing Bad for Science?"

42. Donald J. Waters, "Building on Success, Forging New Ground: The Question of Sustainability," *First Monday* 9, no. 5 (May 3, 2004): 5, https://doi.org/10.5210/fm.v9i5.1148; Judith Ryan et al., "The Future of Scholarly Publishing: MLA Ad Hoc Committee on the Future of Scholarly Publishing," *Profession*, 2002: 172.

43. Gene R. Hawes, *To Advance Knowledge: A Handbook on American University Press Publishing* (New York: American University Press Services, 1967), 127.

44. Nancy L. Maron et al., "The Costs of Publishing Monographs: Toward a Transparent Methodology," white paper, available from Ithaka S + R, 2016, http://www.sr.ithaka.org/publications/the-costs-of-publishing-monographs/

45. Hill Wooldridge & Co. Limited, "Report of the Trustees (Incorporating Strategic Report) and Financial Statements for the Year Ended 31 December 2017 for The Federation of European Biochemical Societies," 2017, accessed November 30, 2019, https://www.febs.org/document-uploads/FEBS_2017_Annual_Report.pdf

46. Rob Johnson and Mattia Fosci, "On Shifting Sands: Assessing the Financial Sustainability of UK Learned Societies," *Learned Publishing* 28, no. 4 (October 1, 2015): 274–82, https://doi.org/10.1087/20150406

47. Rob Johnson and Elle Malcolmson, "You Don't Know What You've Got till It's Gone: The Changing Landscape of UK Learned Society Publishing," *Insights: The UKSG Journal* 37, no. 1 (October 15, 2024): 16.

48. Janet Finch, "Accessibility, Sustainability, Excellence: How to Expand Access to Research Publications," 2012, 11, http://www.researchinfonet.org/wp-content/uploads/2012/06/Finch-Group-report-FINAL-VERSION.pdf

49. RCUK, "RCUK Open Access Policy," 2012, http://www.rcuk.ac.uk/RCUK-prod/assets/documents/documents/RCUKOpenAccessPolicy.pdf

50. Philip Mirowski, "The Evolution of Platform Science," *Social Research: An International Quarterly* 90, no. 4 (December 2023): 733, https://doi.org/10.1353/sor.2023.a916352

51. Massimo De Angelis and Stavros Stavrides, "On the Commons: A Public Interview with Massimo De Angelis and Stavros Stavrides," *E-Flux*, 2010, http://www.e-flux.com/journal/17/67351/on-the-commons-a-public-interview-with-massimo-de-angelis-and-stavros-stavrides/

52. Suber, "Creating an Intellectual Commons."

53. Hess and Ostrom, *Understanding Knowledge*, 3.

54. J. K. Gibson-Graham, Jenny Cameron, and Stephen Healy, "Commoning as Postcapitalist Politics," in *Releasing the Commons: Rethinking the Futures of the Commons*, ed. Ash Amin and Phillip Howel (Oxford: Routledge, 2016), 195.

55. Annemarie Mol, *The Logic of Care: Health and the Problem of Patient Choice* (New York: Routledge, 2008).

56. Joan C. Tronto, *Moral Boundaries: A Political Argument for an Ethic of Care* (New York: Routledge, 1993), 103.

57. Kathleen Fitzpatrick, *Generous Thinking: A Radical Approach to Saving the University* (Baltimore: Johns Hopkins University Press, 2021), 4.

58. Stephen Pinfield, *Achieving Global Open Access: The Need for Scientific, Epistemic and Participatory Openness* (London: Routledge, 2024), 113, https://doi.org/10.4324/9781032679259

59. María Puig de la Bellacasa, *Matters of Care: Speculative Ethics in More than Human Worlds*, Posthumanities 41 (Minneapolis: University of Minnesota Press, 2017), 16.

60. Donna Jeanne Haraway, *Staying with the Trouble: Making Kin in the Chthulucene*, Experimental Futures Technological Lives, Scien-

tific Arts, Anthropological Voices (Durham, NC: Duke University Press, 2016).

61. Haraway, *Staying with the Trouble.*

62. Janneke Adema and Samuel A. Moore, "Collectivity and Collaboration: Imagining New Forms of Communality to Create Resilience in Scholar-Led Publishing," *Insights: The UKSG Journal* 31, no. 1 (2018), https://doi.org/10.1629/uksg.399

63. cOAlition S, "'Plan S' and 'cOAlition S'—Accelerating the Transition to Full and Immediate Open Access to Scientific Publications," 2018, https://www.coalition-s.org/

64. Christopher M. Kelty, *Two Bits: The Cultural Significance of Free Software* (Durham, NC: Duke University Press, 2008).

Chapter 1

1. Roger C. Schonfeld, "Elsevier Acquires Institutional Repository Provider Bepress," *Scholarly Kitchen* (blog), August 2, 2017, https://scholarlykitchen.sspnet.org/2017/08/02/elsevier-acquires-bepress/

2. Sara Leavens, "Penn Libraries to End Partnership with Bepress," *Operation Beprexit* (blog), September 19, 2017, https://beprexit.wordpress.com/official-statement/

3. Cost of Knowledge, "Cost of Knowledge," The Cost of Knowledge, April 2011, http://thecostofknowledge.com/

4. Mélanie Dulong de Rosnay, "Commonswashing by Information Technologies and Online Platforms: The Semantic Appropriation of the Commons," *netCommons* (blog), 2019, https://netcommons.eu/?q=content/commonswashing-information-technologies-and-online-platforms-semantic-appropriation-commons

5. On the commons, "Wrapping Our Legal Minds Around the Global Commons: Res Nullius, Res Communis, and Res Divini Juris," On the commons, 2007, https://web.archive.org/web/20231001004131/http://www.onthecommons.org/wrapping-our-legal-minds-around-global-commons-res-nullius-res-communis-and-res-divini-juris#sthash.fYwHdcfQ.dpbs

6. Jean Birrell, "Common Rights in the Medieval Forest: Disputes

and Conflicts in the Thirteenth Century," *Past & Present*, no. 117 (1987): 22–49.

7. BOAI, "Budapest Open Access Initiative | Ten Years on from the Budapest Open Access Initiative: Setting the Default to Open," Budapest Open Access Initiative, 2012, https://www.budapestopenaccessinitiative.org/boai-10-recommendations

8. "Creative Commons Attribution Licence (CC BY)," Wellcome Trust, accessed August 7, 2024, https://wellcome.org/grant-funding/guidance/open access-guidance/creative-commons-attribution-licence-cc

9. Lawrence Lessig, *The Future of Ideas: The Fate of the Commons in a Connected World* (New York: Random House, 2001).

10. Lessig, 20.

11. Charlotte Hess and Elinor Ostrom, *Understanding Knowledge as a Commons: From Theory to Practice* (Cambridge, MA: MIT Press, 2007), https://doi.org/10.7551/mitpress/6980.001.0001

12. Peter Suber, "Creating an Intellectual Commons through Open Access," in *Understanding Knowledge as a Commons: From Theory to Practice*, ed. Charlotte Hess and Elinor Ostrom (Cambridge, MA: MIT Press, 2007), 9.

13. Lawrence Lessig, *Free Culture: How Big Media Uses Technology and the Law to Lock down Culture and Control Creativity* (New York: Penguin Press, 2004), xvi.

14. Paul Stacey and Sarah Hinchliff Pearson, *Made with Creative Commons* (Copenhagen: Ctrl+Alt+Delete Books, 2017), 14, https://creativecommons.org/wp-content/uploads/2017/04/made-with-cc.pdf

15. Stacey and Pearson, *Made with Creative Commons.*

16. Gary Hall, *Pirate Philosophy: For a Digital Posthumanities* (Cambridge, MA: MIT Press, 2016), 4.

17. Michael Hardt and Antonio Negri, *Commonwealth* (Cambridge, MA: Belknap Press of Harvard University Press, 2009), viii.

18. James Boyle, *The Public Domain: Enclosing the Commons of the Mind* (New Haven: Yale University Press, 2008), 42.

19. Boyle, *Public Domain*, 39.

20. Boyle, *Public Domain*, 40.

21. Boyle, *Public Domain*, 20.

22. Carlo Vercellone, "The Common as a Mode of Production: Towards a Critique of the Political Economy of Common Goods," n.d., http://generation-online.org/c/fc_rent14.htm

23. Vercellone, "The Common."

24. Stephen Buranyi, "Is the Staggeringly Profitable Business of Scientific Publishing Bad for Science?," *The Guardian*, June 27, 2017, sec. Science, http://www.theguardian.com/science/2017/jun/27/profitable-business-scientific-publishing-bad-for-science

25. Vincent Larivière, Stefanie Haustein, and Philippe Mongeon, "The Oligopoly of Academic Publishers in the Digital Era," ed. Wolfgang Glanzel, *PLOS ONE* 10, no. 6 (June 10, 2015): e0127502, https://doi.org/10.1371/journal.pone.0127502

26. Fei Shu et al., "Is It Such a Big Deal? On the Cost of Journal Use in the Digital Era," 2018, https://doi.org/10.5860/crl.79.6.785

27. Peter Suber, *Open Access*, MIT Press Essential Knowledge Series (Cambridge, MA: MIT Press, 2012), 160.

28. OpenAPC, "OpenAPC—Open APC," OpenAPC, no date, https://treemaps.openapc.net/apcdata/openapc/publisher

29. Hess and Ostrom, *Understanding Knowledge as a Commons*, 3.

30. Jason Potts et al., "A Journal Is a Club: A New Economic Model for Scholarly Publishing," *Prometheus*, 2017, 7.

31. Potts et al., "A Journal Is a Club," 11.

32. Leslie Chan and Sely Costa, "Participation in the Global Knowledge Commons: Challenges and Opportunities for Research Dissemination in Developing Countries," *New Library World* 106, no. 3/4 (March 2005): 141–63, https://doi.org/10.1108/03074800510587354; Wendy Leeds-Hurwitz, "Moving (Slowly) toward Understanding Knowledge as a Global Commons," *Journal of Multicultural Discourses*, November 28, 2019, 1–8, https://doi.org/10.1080/17447143.2019.1695806

33. Heather Morrison, "About Sustaining the Knowledge Commons / À Propos Des Savoirs Communs," Sustaining the Knowledge Commons / Soutenir les savoirs communs, June 23, 2014, https://sustainingknowledgecommons.org/about/

34. Morrison, "About Sustaining the Knowledge Commons."

35. Jeroen Bosman et al., "The Scholarly Commons—Principles and

Practices to Guide Research Communication" (Open Science Framework, 2017), 3, https://osf.io/6c2xt/

36. Bosman et al., "The Scholarly Commons," 13.

37. Silvia, Federici, *Caliban and the Witch* (New York: Autonomedia, 2004), 26.

38. Federici, *Caliban*, 101.

39. Birrell, "Common Rights in the Medieval Forest," 23.

40. Peter Linebaugh, *The Magna Carta Manifesto: Liberties and Commons for All* (Berkeley: University of California Press, 2008), 49.

41. José Esteban Muñoz, *The Sense of Brown*, ed. Tavia Amolo Ochieng' Nyongó and Joshua Takano Chambers-Letson, Perverse Modernities (Durham: Duke University Press, 2020), 4.

42. Hess and Ostrom, *Understanding Knowledge as a Commons*, 67.

43. Elsa Noterman, "Beyond Tragedy: Differential Commoning in a Manufactured Housing Cooperative: Beyond Tragedy," *Antipode* 48, no. 2 (March 2016): 433–52, https://doi.org/10.1111/anti.12182; Daniel Parris and Miriam Williams, "Care-Full Commoning at the Old Church on the Hill, Bendigo," *Australian Geographer* 50, no. 4 (October 2, 2019): 531–46, https://doi.org/10.1080/00049182.2019.1682289; Julia Udall, "Mending the Commons with the 'Little Mesters,'" *Ephemera: Theory & Politics in Organization*, 2019, 29.

44. Patrick Bresnihan, "The More-than-Human Commons: From Commons to Commoning," in *Space, Power and the Commons: The Struggle for Alternative Futures* (New York: Routledge, 2016).

45. Patrick Bresnihan, *Transforming the Fisheries: Neoliberalism, Nature, and the Commons* (Lincoln: University of Nebraska Press, 2016), 128.

46. Stefano Harney et al., *All Incomplete* (Colchester: Minor Compositions, 2021), 129.

47. Christian Fuchs and Marisol Sandoval, "The Diamond Model of Open Access Publishing: Why Policy Makers, Scholars, Universities, Libraries, Labour Unions and the Publishing World Need to Take Non-Commercial, Non-Profit Open Access Serious," *tripleC: Communication, Capitalism & Critique. Open Access Journal for a Global Sustainable Information Society* 13, no. 2 (2013): 429.

48. Suber, *Open Access*, 10.

49. Massimo De Angelis and Stavros Stavrides, "On the Commons: A Public Interview with Massimo De Angelis and Stavros Stavrides," *E-Flux*, 2010, http://www.e-flux.com/journal/17/67351/on-the-commons-a-public-interview-with-massimo-de-angelis-and-stavros-stavrides/

50. De Angelis and Stavrides, "On the Commons."

51. J. K. Gibson-Graham, Jenny Cameron, and Stephen Healy, "Commoning as Postcapitalist Politics," in *Releasing the Commons: Rethinking the Futures of the Commons*, ed. Ash Amin and Phillip Howel (Oxford: Routledge, 2016), 207.

52. David Fagundes, "Labor and/as Love: Exploring the Commons of Roller Derby," in *Governing Knowledge Commons*, ed. Brett M. Frischmann, Michael J. Madison, and Katherine J. Strandburg (Oxford: Oxford University Press, 2014), 417–44.

53. Dulong de Rosnay, "Commonswashing."

54. See Moore, "A Genealogy of Open Access: Negotiations between Openness and Access to Research," *Revue Française Des Sciences de l'information et de La Communication*, no. 11 (2017), https://doi.org/10.4000/rfsic.3220, for an overview of the various lineages of the open access movement.

55. See Janet Finch, "Accessibility, Sustainability, Excellence: How to Expand Access to Research Publications," Report, 2012, 69, http://www.researchinfonet.org/wp-content/uploads/2012/06/Finch-Group-report-FINAL-VERSION.pdf, for evidence of this argument.

56. Lisa Matthias, "The Worst of Both Worlds: Hybrid Open Access," OpenAIRE, 2018, https://www.openaire.eu/blogs/the-worst-of-both-worlds-hybrid-open access

57. Vercellone, "The Common."

58. Hess and Ostrom, *Understanding Knowledge as a Commons*.

Chapter 2

1. ROARMAP, "Browse by Country," accessed May 8, 2020, http://roarmap.eprints.org/view/country/un=5Fgeoscheme.html

2. Peter Suber, "The Taxpayer Argument for Open Access," *SPARC*

Open Access Newsletter, 2003, https://dash.harvard.edu/bitstream/handle/1/4725013/suber_taxpayer.htm

3. Samuel A. Moore, "Open Access, Plan S and 'Radically Liberatory' Forms of Academic Freedom," *Development and Change* 52, no. 6 (January 29, 2021), https://doi.org/10.1111/dech.12640

4. Janet Finch, "Accessibility, Sustainability, Excellence: How to Expand Access to Research Publications," Report, 2012, unpaginated, http://www.researchinfonet.org/wp-content/uploads/2012/06/Finch-Group-report-FINAL-VERSION.pdf

5. David Willetts, "Public Access to Publicly-Funded Research," GOV.UK, May 2, 2012, https://www.gov.uk/government/speeches/public-access-to-publicly-funded-research

6. Willetts, "Public Access."

7. Finch, "Accessibility, Sustainability, Excellence."

8. RCUK, "RCUK Open Access Policy," 2012, http://www.rcuk.ac.uk/RCUK-prod/assets/documents/documents/RCUKOpenAccessPolicy.pdf

9. Janneke Adema and Samuel A. Moore, "Scaling Small; Or How to Envision New Relationalities for Knowledge Production," *Westminster Papers in Communication and Culture* 16, no. 1 (March 22, 2021), https://doi.org/10.16997/wpcc.918; Martin Paul Eve and Jonathan Gray, eds., *Reassembling Scholarly Communications: Histories, Infrastructures, and Global Politics of Open Access* (Cambridge, MA: MIT Press, 2020), https://doi.org/10.7551/mitpress/11885.001.0001

10. Science Europe, "Open Access," Science Europe, 2018, https://www.scienceeurope.org/our-priorities/open-access/

11. cOAlition S, "'Plan S' and 'cOAlition S'—Accelerating the Transition to Full and Immediate Open Access to Scientific Publications," 2018, https://www.coalition-s.org/

12. Coalition S, "Plan S Principles," Plan S, accessed August 12, 2024, https://www.coalition-s.org/plan_s_principles/

13. Robert-Jan Smits and Rachael Pells, *Plan S for Shock: Science. Shock. Solution. Speed* (Ubiquity Press, 2022), 48, https://doi.org/10.5334/bcq

14. Smits and Pells, *Plan S for Shock*, 85.

15. Smits and Pells, *Plan S for Shock*, 111.

16. STM Association, "STM Statement on Plan S: Accelerating the Transition to Full and Immediate Open Access to Scientific Publications," 2018, https://www.stm-assoc.org/2018_09_04_STM_Statement_on_PlanS.pdf

17. Michael Clarke, "Plan S: Impact on Society Publishers," *Scholarly Kitchen*, December 5, 2018, https://scholarlykitchen.sspnet.org/2018/12/05/plan-s-impact-on-society-publishers/

18. Jack Grove, "Elsevier and Springer Nature Sit Out Plan S Cost Comparison Tool," *Times Higher Education*, November 16, 2022, https://www.timeshighereducation.com/news/elsevier-and-springer-nature-sit-out-plan-s-cost-comparison-tool

19. Smits and Pells, *Plan S for Shock*, 85.

20. Alexander Grossmann and Björn Brembs, "Current Market Rates for Scholarly Publishing Services" (F1000Research, July 1, 2021), https://doi.org/10.12688/f1000research.27468.2

21. Christina Garsten and Monica Lindh De Montoya, eds., *Transparency in a New Global Order: Unveiling Organizational Visions* (Cheltenham, UK: Edward Elgar, 2008), 3.

22. Clare Birchall, "Radical Transparency?" *Cultural Studies ↔ Critical Methodologies* 14, no. 1 (February 2014): 77–88, https://doi.org/10.1177/1532708613517442

23. Michel Foucault, *The Birth of Biopolitics: Lectures at the Collège de France, 1978–79*, trans. Michel Senellart (Basingstoke, UK: Palgrave Macmillan, 2008), 226.

24. Eduardo Aguado-López and Arianna Becerril-Garcia, "AmeliCA before Plan S—The Latin American Initiative to Develop a Cooperative, Non-Commercial, Academic Led, System of Scholarly Communication," *Impact of Social Sciences* (blog), August 8, 2019, https://blogs.lse.ac.uk/impactofsocialsciences/2019/08/08/amelica-before-plan-s-the-latin-american-initiative-to-develop-a-cooperative-non-commercial-academic-led-system-of-scholarly-communication/

25. cOAlition S, "Rationale for the Revisions Made to the Plan S Principles and Implementation Guidance | Plan S," Plan S, 2019, https://www.coalition-s.org/rationale-for-the-revisions/

26. Holly Else, "Ambitious Open-Access Plan S Delayed to Let Research Community Adapt," *Nature*, May 30, 2019, https://doi.org/10.1038/d41586-019-01717-2

27. "From Principles to Implementation: cOAlition S Releases Implementation Guidance on Plan S | Plan S," accessed June 25, 2023, https://www.coalition-s.org/implementation-guidance-on-plan-s-now-open-for-public-feedback/

28. Michel Callon, "Some Elements of a Sociology of Translation: Domestication of the Scallops and the Fishermen of St Brieuc Bay," *Sociological Review* 32, no. S1 (1984): 196–233.

29. Margot Finn, "Royal Historical Society Guidance Paper" (Royal Historical Society, 2019), https://files.royalhistsoc.org/wp-content/uploads/2019/10/17204855/RHS_PlanS_Full_Report_Oct19_FINAL.pdf; Shina Caroline Lynn Kamerlin et al., "Journal Open Access and Plan S: Solving Problems or Shifting Burdens?" *Development and Change* 52, no. 3 (2021): 627–50, https://doi.org/10.1111/dech.12635

30. Rick Anderson, "Open Access and Academic Freedom: Teasing Out Some Important Nuances," *Development and Change* 52, no. 6 (2021): 1503–12, https://doi.org/10.1111/dech.12636

31. cOAlition S, "Plan S Rights Retention Strategy." Accessed January 31, 2023, https://www.coalition-s.org/rights-retention-strategy/

32. Rachel Magee, "Manuscripts 'Rejected' for Using Rights Retention Statements," *Research Professional*, 2022, https://www.researchprofessional.com/0/rr/news/uk/open-access/2022/10/Manuscripts--rejected--for-using-rights-retention-statements.html?utm_medium=email&utm_source=rpMailing&utm_campaign=personalNewsDailyUpdate_2022-10-11

33. Annemarie Mol, *The Logic of Care: Health and the Problem of Patient Choice* (New York: Routledge, 2008), 18.

34. Mol, *The Logic of Care*, 57.

35. Sally Rumsey, "Springer Nature Doublespeak," *Soapbox* (blog), 2022, https://www.coalition-s.org/blog/springer-nature-doublespeak/

36. Björn Brembs et al., "Creating a Market to Replace Publisher Monopolies | Plan S," *Soapbox* (blog), 2022, https://www.coalition-s.org/blog/creating-a-market-to-replace-publisher-monopolies/

37. Rob Johnson, "From Coalition to Commons: Plan S and the Future of Scholarly Communication," *Insights: The UKSG Journal* 32 (January 30, 2019), https://doi.org/10.1629/uksg.453

38. Johnson, "From Coalition to Commons," 2.

39. Mol, *The Logic of Care*, 18.

40. Samuel A. Moore, "Reflections on Research Assessment #1: Samuel Moore on 'Research Assessment in the University without Condition,'" Billet, *DARIAH Open* (blog), October 10, 2022, https://dariahopen.hypotheses.org/1527

41. Research Whisperer, "Open Access at No Cost? Just Ditch Academic Journals," *Research Whisperer* (blog), June 21, 2021, https://researchwhisperer.org/2021/06/22/open-access-at-no-cost/.

42. Rob Johnson, "Operationalising Open Research Europe as a Collective Publishing Enterprise—Case Study: SCOAP3" (Zenodo, October 24, 2022), https://doi.org/10.5281/zenodo.7258539

43. Elea Giménez Toledo et al., "Bibliodiversity—What It Is and Why It Is Essential to Creating Situated Knowledge," *Impact of Social Sciences* (blog), December 5, 2019, https://blogs.lse.ac.uk/impactofsocialsciences/2019/12/05/bibliodiversity-what-it-is-and-why-it-is-essential-to-creating-situated-knowledge/

44. Maria Mies, "No Commons without a Community," *Community Development Journal* 49, suppl_1 (January 1, 2014): i106–i117, https://doi.org/10.1093/cdj/bsu007

45. Susan Leigh Star and Anselm Strauss, "Layers of Silence, Arenas of Voice: The Ecology of Visible and Invisible Work," *Computer Supported Cooperative Work (CSCW)* 8, no. 1–2 (1999): 15.

46. Star and Strauss, "Layers of Silence," 17.

47. Aloha Record and Ravonne Green, "Examining Gender Issues and Trends in Library Management from the Male Perspective," *Library Leadership & Management* 22, no. 4 (2008): 193–98.

48. Kim England, fHome, Work and the Shifting Geographies of Care," *Ethics, Place & Environment* 13, no. 2 (June 2010): 133, https://doi.org/10.1080/13668791003778826

49. Roxanne Shirazi, "Reproducing the Academy: Librarians and the Question of Service in the Digital Humanities," in *Making Things and*

Drawing Boundaries: Experiments in the Digital Humanities, ed. Jentery Sayers (Minneapolis: University of Minnesota Press, 2018).

50. Silvia Federici, *Caliban and the Witch* (New York: Autonomedia, 2004), 97.

51. Stefano Harney and Fred Moten, *The Undercommons: Fugitive Planning & Black Study* (Wivenhoe: Minor Compositions, 2013), 26.

52. Samuel A. Moore, "A Genealogy of Open Access: Negotiations between Openness and Access to Research," *Revue Française Des Sciences de l'information et de La Communication*, no. 11 (2017), https://doi.org/10.4000/rfsic.3220

53. Rachel Magee, "EU Ready to Back Immediate Open Access without Author Fees," *Research Professional News* (blog), May 5, 2023, https://www.researchprofessionalnews.com/rr-news-europe-infrastructure-2023-5-eu-ready-to-back-immediate-open-access-without-author-fees/.

Chapter 3

1. Gowan Dawson and Jonathan R. Topham, "Introduction," in *Science Periodicals in Nineteenth-Century Britain: Constructing Scientific Communities*, ed. Gowan Dawson et al. (Chicago: University of Chicago Press, 2020), 20, https://doi.org/10.7208/chicago/9780226683461.001.0001

2. Aileen Fyfe et al., *A History of Scientific Journals* (London: UCL Press, 2022), 492, https://doi.org/10.14324/111.9781800082328

3. Even the editorial content of publications is now increasingly subject to censorship and editorial restrictions by publishing houses, particularly relating to the commercial need to appease surveillant and repressive governments.

4. Jack Grove, "Journal Resignations 'Can Drive Scholar-Led Publishing Revolution,'" *Times Higher Education (THE)*, June 8, 2023, https://www.timeshighereducation.com/news/journal-resignations-can-drive-scholar-led-publishing-revolution

5. Anna Fazackerley, "'Too Greedy': Mass Walkout at Global Science Journal over 'Unethical' Fees," *The Observer*, May 7, 2023, sec. Science,

https://www.theguardian.com/science/2023/may/07/too-greedy-mass-walkout-at-global-science-journal-over-unethical-fees

6. Judith Green and Lindsay McLaren, "Resignation Letter," CPHN, July 5, 2023, https://cphn.net/2023/07/05/resignation-letter/

7. Green and McLaren, "Resignation Letter."

8. Raymond Williams, *Keywords: A Vocabulary of Culture and Society* (New York: Oxford University Press, 1976), 76.

9. Tobias Steiner, "Lost in Translation? Revisiting Notions of Community- and Scholar-Led Publishing in International Contexts," *Scholar-Led* (blog), 2023, https://flavoursofopen.science/lost-in-translation-revisiting-notions-of-community-and-scholar-led-publishing-in-international-contexts/

10. Melanie Schlosser and Catherine Mitchell, "Academy-Owned? Academic-Led? Community-Led? What's at Stake in the Words We Use to Describe New Publishing Paradigms," *Library Publishing Coalition Blog* (blog), accessed November 28, 2019, https://librarypublishing.org/alpd19-academy-owned-academic-led-community-led/

11. Steiner, "Lost in Translation?"

12. Marcel Wrzesinski, "Reclaiming (Parts of) Scholarly Communication: Resilient Publishing as a Community-Driven Effort," *Weizenbaum Journal of the Digital Society* 3, no. 2 (October 30, 2023), https://doi.org/10.34669/wi.wjds/3.2.5

13. Tim Berners-Lee, "WorldWideWeb: Summary," 1991, https://www.w3.org/People/Berners-Lee/1991/08/art-6487.txt

14. Stevan Harnad, "The 1994 'Subversive Proposal' at 10," June 27, 2004, https://web.archive.org/web/20120216132821/http://listserver.sigmaxi.org/sc/wa.exe?A2=ind04&L=american-scientist-open-access-forum&D=1&O=D&F=l&S=&P=58204

15. Paul Ginsparg, "It Was Twenty Years Ago Today . . . ," *arXiv*, 2011, http://arxiv.org/abs/1108.2700

16. Charles W. Bailey Jr., "Libraries with Glass Walls," *Public-Access Computer Systems Review* 1, no. 2 (1990), https://journals.tdl.org/pacsr/index.php/pacsr/article/view/5961/5593

17. James J O'Donnell, "Five Years of Bryn Mawr Classical Review," *The Serials Librarian: From the Printed Page to the Digital Age* 28, no. 3–4 (1996): 227, https://doi.org/10.1300/J123v28n03_04

18. O'Donnell, "Five Years," 227.

19. Eyal Amiran and John Unsworth, "Postmodern Culture: Publishing in the Electronic Medium," *The Public-Access Computer Systems Review* 2, no. 1 (1991): unpaginated, https://journals.tdl.org/pacsr/index.php/pacsr/article/view/6025

20. Eyal Amiran, "The Rhetoric of Serials at the Present Time," *The Serials Librarian* 28, no. 3–4 (April 22, 1996): unpaginated, https://doi.org/10.1300/J123v28n03_03

21. Steve Hitchcock, Les Carr, and Wendy Hall, "A Survey of STM Online Journals 1990–95: The Calm Before the Storm," The Open Journal Project, 1996, https://web-archive.southampton.ac.uk/journals.ecs.soton.ac.uk/survey/survey.html

22. Rebekka Kiesewetter, "Undoing Scholarship: Towards an Activist Genealogy of the OA Movement," Tijdschrift voor Genderstudies 23, no. 2 (2020): 18.

23. Andrew M Odlyzko, "Tragic Loss or Good Riddance? The Impending Demise of Traditional Scholarly Journals" 42, no. 1 (1995): 52.

24. Stevan Harnad, "For Whom the Gate Tolls? From Stevan Harnad," *American-Scientist-Open-Access-Forum*, 1998, http://users.ecs.soton.ac.uk/harnad/Hypermail/Amsci/0001.html

25. Samuel A. Moore, "Revisiting 'the 1990s Debutante': Scholar-Led Publishing and the Prehistory of the Open Access Movement," *Journal of the Association for Information Science and Technology* 71, no. 7 (2020), https://doi.org/10.1002/asi.24306; Christopher M. Kelty, *Two Bits: The Cultural Significance of Free Software* (Durham, NC: Duke University Press, 2008).

26. Janneke Adema, Graham Stone, and Chris Keene, "Changing Publishing Ecologies: A Landscape Study of New University Presses and Academic-Led Publishing," 2017, http://repository.jisc.ac.uk/6666/1/Changing-publishing-ecologies-report.pdf

27. Janneke Adema, "Interview Transcriptions: Changing Publishing Ecologies. A Landscape Study of New University Presses and Academic-Led Publishing," 2017, http://repository.jisc.ac.uk/6652/

28. Adema, Stone, and Keene, "Changing Publishing Ecologies," 3.

29. Mercedes Bunz, interview with Mercedes Bunz of Meson Press, interview by Janneke Adema, 2017, 1, http://repository.jisc.ac.uk/6652/

30. Craig Saper, interview with Craig Saper of Roving Eye Press and Electric Press, interview by Janneke Adema, 2017, 1, http://repository.jisc.ac.uk/6652/; Kathleen Fitzpatrick, interview with Kathleen Fitzpatrick of Media Commons Press, interview by Janneke Adema, 2017, 1, http://repository.jisc.ac.uk/6652/

31. Stephen Connelly, interview with Stephen Connelly of Counter Press, interview by Janneke Adema, 2017, 1, http://repository.jisc.ac.uk/6652/

32. Joe Deville, interview with Joe Deville of Mattering Press, interview by Janneke Adema, 2017, 1, http://repository.jisc.ac.uk/6652/; Chris Land, interview of Chris Land, MayFly Books, interview by Janneke Adema, 2017, 1, http://repository.jisc.ac.uk/6652/

33. Andrea E. Pia et al., "Labour of Love: An Open Access Manifesto for Freedom, Integrity, and Creativity in the Humanities and Interpretive Social Sciences," *Commonplace*, July 16, 2020, https://doi.org/10.21428/6ffd8432.a7503356

34. Sebastian Nordhoff, interview with Sebastian Nordhoff of Language Science Press, interview by Janneke Adema, 2017, 1, http://repository.jisc.ac.uk/6652/

35. Land, interview, 1.

36. Rupert Gatti, interview with Rupert Gatti of Open Book Publishers, interview by Janneke Adema, 2017, 1, http://repository.jisc.ac.uk/6652/

37. Eileen Joy, interview with Eileen Joy of punctum books, interview by Janneke Adema, 2017, 11–12, http://repository.jisc.ac.uk/6652/

38. Fitzpatrick, interview.

39. Open Humanities Press, interview with Open Humanities Press, interview by Janneke Adema, 2017, 4, http://repository.jisc.ac.uk/6652/

40. Land, interview, 6.

41. Joy, interview, 2.

42. Jacques Derrida, "The Future of the Profession or the Unconditional University (Thanks to the Humanities That Could Take Place Tomorrow)," in *Jacques Derrida and the Humanities: A Critical Reader*, ed. Tom Cohen (Cambridge: Cambridge University Press, 2001), 26.

43. Connelly, interview, 7.

44. Land, interview, 4.

45. Joy, interview, 4.

46. Land, interview, 6.

47. Ernesto Laclau, "Ethics, Politics and Radical Democracy—A Response to Simon Critchley," *Culture Machine* 4 (2002), https://culturemachine.net/the-ethico-political-issue/ethics-politics-a-response-to-simon-critchley/

48. Jacques Derrida, *The Other Heading Reflections on Today's Europe*, trans. Pascale Anne Braut and Michael B. Naas (Bloomington: Indiana University Press, 1992), 24.

49. Deville, interview, 2–3.

50. Joan C. Tronto, *Moral Boundaries: A Political Argument for an Ethic of Care* (New York: Routledge, 1993), 103.

51. María Puig de la Bellacasa, *Matters of Care: Speculative Ethics in More than Human Worlds*, Posthumanities 41 (Minneapolis: University of Minnesota Press, 2017), 6.

52. Sebastian Abrahamsson et al., "Mattering Press—New Forms of Care for STS Books," 2013, https://www.matteringpress.org/blog/new-forms-of-care-for-sts-books

53. Andy Tattersall, "For What It's Worth—the Open Peer Review Landscape," ed. Professor G.E. Gorman and Professor Jennifer, *Online Information Review* 39, no. 5 (September 14, 2015): 649–63, https://doi.org/10.1108/OIR-06-2015-0182

54. Open Humanities Press, interview, 2.

55. Joy, interview; Deville, interview, 2.

56. Annemarie Mol, *The Logic of Care: Health and the Problem of Patient Choice* (New York: Routledge, 2008), 14.

57. Mol, *The Logic of Care*, 58–59.

58. Bunz, interview.

59. Open Humanities Press, interview.

60. Gatti, interview.

61. Sarah Kember, interview with Sarah Kember of Goldsmiths Press, interview by Janneke Adema, 2017, 1, http://repository.jisc.ac.uk/6652/

62. Sarah Kember, "At Risk? The Humanities and the Future of Academic Publishing," *Journal of Electronic Publishing* 19, no. 2 (Fall 2016), http://dx.doi.org/10.3998/3336451.0019.210

63. Land, interview, 2.

64. Joy, interview, 4.

65. Michel Foucault, *Care of the Self: The History of Sexuality*, Vol. 3, trans. Robert Hurley (London: Penguin Books, 1984).

66. Foucault, *Care of the Self*, 53.

67. Joy, interview, 4.

68. Massimo De Angelis, *Omnia Sunt Communia: On the Commons and the Transformation to Postcapitalism* (London: Zed Books, 2017).

69. Guilherme Fians, "Prefigurative Politics," in *Open Encyclopedia of Anthropology*, 2022, https://www.anthroencyclopedia.com/entry/prefigurative-politics

70. George Caffentzis, "A Tale of Two Conferences: Globalization, the Crisis of Neoliberalism and Question of the Commons," *Centre for Global Justice*, 2004. https://www.globaljusticecenter.org/papers/tale-two-conferences-globalization-crisis-neoliberalism-and-question-commons

71. Janneke Adema and Samuel A. Moore, "'Just One Day of Unstructured Autonomous Time': Samuel A. Moore Supporting Editorial Labour for Ethical Publishing within the University," *New Formations* 110 (2024): 8–27, https://doi.org/10.3898/NewF:110-111.01.2024

72. Janneke Adema, *Living Books: Experiments in the Posthumanities* (Cambridge, MA: MIT Press, 2022), 159.

73. Chantal Mouffe, *Agonistics: Thinking the World Politically* (London: Verso, 2013), 91.

74. Mouffe, Agonistics, 88.

75. Mouffe, Agonistics, 95.

76. Mouffe, Agonistics, 98.

77. Mouffe, Agonistics, 100.

78. Kember, interview, 1.

Chapter 4

1. Alejandro Posada and George Chen, "Inequality in Knowledge Production: The Integration of Academic Infrastructure by Big Publishers," in *22nd International Conference on Electronic Publishing* (Mar-

seille: OpenEdition Press, 2018), https://doi.org/10.4000/proceedings.elpub.2018.30

2. Samuel A. Moore, "Individuation through Infrastructure: *Get Full Text Research*, Data Extraction and the Academic Publishing Oligopoly," *Journal of Documentation* (July 28, 2020), https://doi.org/10.1108/JD-06-2020-0090

3. Roger Schonfeld, "The Supercontinent of Scholarly Publishing?" *Scholarly Kitchen* (blog), May 3, 2018, https://scholarlykitchen.sspnet.org/2018/05/03/supercontinent-scholarly-publishing/

4. Sarah Lamdan, *Data Cartels: The Companies That Control and Monopolize Our Information* (Stanford, CA: Stanford University Press, 2023), 65.

5. Nick Couldry and Ulises Ali Mejias, *The Costs of Connection: How Data Is Colonizing Human Life and Appropriating It for Capitalism*, (Stanford, CA: Stanford University Press, 2019.

6. Couldry and Mejias, *Costs of Connection*, 33.

7. Simon Batterbury, Gerda Wielander, and Andrea E. Pia, "After the Labour of Love: The Incomplete Revolution of Open Access and Open Science in the Humanities and Creative Social Sciences," *Commonplace*, May 6, 2022, https://doi.org/10.21428/6ffd8432.5e24d46d

8. Arianna Becerril , et al., "OA Diamond Journals Study. Part 2: Recommendations" (Zenodo, March 9, 2021), https://doi.org/10.5281/ZENODO.4562790

9. https://diamasproject.eu/objectives/

10. Katharine Sanderson, "EU Council's 'No Pay' Publishing Model Draws Mixed Response," *Nature*, June 2, 2023, https://doi.org/10.1038/d41586-023-01810-7

11. Johan Rooryck and Pierre Mounier, "D.1.3 Towards an Enhanced and Aligned Institutional Publishing Landscape in the ERA," August 1, 2023, https://doi.org/10.5281/ZENODO.8202169

12. Arianna Becerril et al., "OA Diamond Journals Study. Part 2," 23.

13. J. Britt Holbrook, "Concerning CC BY Mandates, Part 2," *Jbrittholbrook* (blog), December 17, 2018, https://jbrittholbrook.com/2018/12/17/concerning-cc-by-mandates-part-2/

14. A collective of feminist and social justice editors, "After Open

Access," *Critical Legal Thinking* (blog), July 15, 2020, https://criticallegalthinking.com/2020/07/15/after-open-access/

15. Lauren Gail Berlant, *On the Inconvenience of Other People*, Writing Matters! (Durham: Duke University Press, 2022).

16. Berlant. *On the Inconvenience of Other People*.

17. Susan Leigh Star, "The Ethnography of Infrastructure," *American Behavioral Scientist* 43, no. 3 (1999): 382, https://doi.org/10.1177/00027649921955326

18. Star, "Ethnography," 386.

19. Oya Y. Rieger and Roger Schonfeld, "Common Scholarly Communication Infrastructure Landscape Review" (Ithaka S+R, April 24, 2023), https://doi.org/10.18665/sr.318775; Björn Brembs et al., "Replacing Academic Journals," *Royal Society Open Science* 10, no. 7 (July 19, 2023): 230206, https://doi.org/10.1098/rsos.230206

20. Jonathan Gray, "Infrastructural Experiments and the Politics of Open Access," in *Reassembling Scholarly Communications: Histories, Infrastructures, and Global Politics of Open Access*, ed. Martin Paul Eve and Jonathan Gray (Cambridge, MA: MIT Press, 2020), 257.

21. Janneke Adema and Samuel A. Moore, "Collectivity and Collaboration: Imagining New Forms of Communality to Create Resilience in Scholar-Led Publishing," *Insights: The UKSG Journal* 31, no. 1 (2018), https://doi.org/10.1629/uksg.399

22. http://radicaloa.disruptivemedia.org.uk/philosophy/

23. Janneke Adema, *Living Books: Experiments in the Posthumanities* (Cambridge, MA: MIT Press, 2022).

24. Janneke Adema and Samuel A. Moore, "Scaling Small; Or How to Envision New Relationalities for Knowledge Production," *Westminster Papers in Communication and Culture* 16, no. 1 (March 22, 2021), https://doi.org/10.16997/wpcc.918

25. Anna Lowenhaupt Tsing, *The Mushroom at the End of the World: On the Possibility of Life in Capitalist Ruins* (Princeton, NJ: Princeton University Press, 2017), 135.

26. Stefano Harney and Fred Moten, *The Undercommons: Fugitive Planning & Black Study* (Wivenhoe: Minor Compositions, 2013).

27. Femke Snelting and Elodie Mugrefya, "CC4r * COLLECTIVE

CONDITIONS FOR RE-USE," 2023, https://constantvzw.org/wefts/cc4r.en.html

28. Hanna Rebekka Kiesewetter, "Reading Differently: Expanding Open Access Definitions Towards Greater Knowledge Equity" (Coventry University, 2023), 15, https://pure.coventry.ac.uk/ws/portalfiles/portal/78391764/ReadingDifferently_Final_RebekkaKiesewetter_lib_1_.pdf

29. Elea Giménez Toledo et al., "Bibliodiversity—What It Is and Why It Is Essential to Creating Situated Knowledge," *Impact of Social Sciences* (blog), December 5, 2019, https://blogs.lse.ac.uk/impactofsocialsciences/2019/12/05/bibliodiversity-what-it-is-and-why-it-is-essential-to-creating-situated-knowledge/

30. A. L. Tsing, "On Nonscalability: The Living World Is Not Amenable to Precision-Nested Scales," *Common Knowledge* 18, no. 3 (October 1, 2012): 505–24, https://doi.org/10.1215/0961754X-1630424

31. Tsing, "On Nonscalability," 507.

32. Tsing, "On Nonscalability," 42.

33. Adema and Moore, "Scaling Small."

34. Massimo De Angelis, *Omnia Sunt Communia: On the Commons and the Transformation to Postcapitalism* (London: Zed Books, 2017), 287.

35. De Angelis, *Omnia Sunt Communia*, 267.

36. Richard Poynder, "Open Access: 'Information Wants to Be Free'?" *Open and Shut* (blog), 2020, https://poynder.blogspot.com/2020/12/open-access-information-wants-to-be-free.html

37. Adema, *Living Books*, 173.

38. https://scalingsmall.pubpub.org/

39. https://openbookcollective.org/cms/fixed_page/governance/

40. https://www.openingthefuture.net/

41. https://thoth.pub/

42. Humanities Commons, "Sustaining the Commons," accessed July 26, 2024, https://sustaining.hcommons.org/

43. Arianna Becerril-García and Eduardo Aguado-López, "Redalyc—AmeliCA: A Non-Profit Publishing Model to Preserve the Scholary and Open Nature of Scientific Communication" (United Nations Educational, Scientific and Cultural Organization; Latin American Council of Social

Sciences; Network of Scientific Journals from Latin America and the Caribbean, Spain and Portugal; Autonomous University of the State of Mexico; National University of La Plata; University of Antioquia, 2019), http://web.archive.org/web/20220121144814/http://www.amelica.org/wp-content/uploads/2019/04/proyecto-en-extenso-AmeliCA-eng.pdf; Abel L. Packer and Dominique Babini, "The Pasts, Presents, and Futures of SciELO," in *Reassembling Scholarly Communications*, ed. Martin Paul Eve and Jonathan Gray (Cambridge, MA: MIT Press, 2020), 297–314, https://doi.org/10.7551/mitpress/11885.003.0030

44. Phillip A. Sharp et al., "Access to Science and Scholarship: Key Questions about the Future of Research Publishing" (MIT report v1.5, 2023), 41, https://access-to-science.pubpub.org/

45. Leslie Chan et al., "Open Science Beyond Open Access: For and with Communities, A Step towards the Decolonization of Knowledge" (Ottawa: Canadian Commission for UNESCO, July 15, 2020), https://doi.org/10.5281/zenodo.3946773

46. Kiesewetter, "Reading Differently," 143.

47. Chantal Mouffe, *Agonistics: Thinking the World Politically* (London: Verso, 2013), 98.

48. Sarah Kember and Joanna Zylinska, *Life after New Media: Mediation as a Vital Process* (Cambridge, MA: MIT Press, 2012).

49. Adema, *Living Books*, 161.

50. Berlant, *On the Inconvenience of Other People*.

Conclusion

1. Stefano Harney and Fred Moten, *The Undercommons: Fugitive Planning & Black Study* (Wivenhoe: Minor Compositions, 2013).

2. Mark A. Hanson et al., "The Strain on Scientific Publishing" (arXiv, September 27, 2023), https://doi.org/10.48550/arXiv.2309.15884

3. Ellie Kincaid, "Wiley to Stop Using 'Hindawi' Name amid $18 Million Revenue Decline," *Retraction Watch* (blog), December 6, 2023, https://retractionwatch.com/2023/12/06/wiley-to-stop-using-hindawi-name-amid-18-million-revenue-decline/

4. Samuel A. Moore, "The Politics of Rights Retention," *Publications* 11, no. 2 (June 2023): 28, https://doi.org/10.3390/publications11020028

5. "Open Access Accord 'to Weaken Publishers' Negotiating Position,'" *Times Higher Education*, January 23, 2023, https://www.timeshighereducation.com/news/open-access-accord-weaken-publishers-negotiating-position

6. Thomas Hervé Mboa Nkoudou, "Epistemic Alienation in African Scholarly Communications: Open Access as a Pharmakon," in *Reassembling Scholarly Communications*, ed. Martin Paul Eve and Jonathan Gray (Cambridge, MA: MIT Press, 2020), 25–40, https://doi.org/10.7551/mitpress/11885.003.0006

7. Mboa Nkoudou, "Epistemic Alienation," 33.

8. Samuel A. Moore, "Community Governance in Scholarly Communication" (Zenodo, August 30, 2022), https://zenodo.org/record/7034521

9. Michael Max Bühler et al., "Unlocking the Power of Digital Commons: Data Cooperatives as a Pathway for Data Sovereign, Innovative and Equitable Digital Communities," SSRN Scholarly Paper (Rochester, NY, June 29, 2023), https://papers.ssrn.com/abstract=4537273

10. Charlotte Hess and Elinor Ostrom, *Understanding Knowledge as a Commons: From Theory to Practice* (Cambridge, MA: MIT Press, 2007), 67, http://public.eblib.com/choice/publicfullrecord.aspx?p=3338502

11. http://thecostofknowledge.com/

12. Tom Heyman, Pieter Moors, and Gert Storms, "On the Cost of Knowledge: Evaluating the Boycott against Elsevier," *Frontiers in Research Metrics and Analytics* 1 (October 17, 2016), https://doi.org/10.3389/frma.2016.00007

13. Massimo De Angelis and Stavros Stavrides, "On the Commons: A Public Interview with Massimo De Angelis and Stavros Stavrides," *E-Flux*, 2010, http://www.e-flux.com/journal/17/67351/on-the-commons-a-public-interview-with-massimo-de-angelis-and-stavros-stavrides/

14. Katharine Sanderson, "Editors Quit Top Neuroscience Journal to Protest against Open-Access Charges," *Nature* 616, no. 7958 (April 21,

2023): 641, https://doi.org/10.1038/d41586-023-01391-5; Judith Green and Lindsay McLaren, "Resignation Letter," CPHN, July 5, 2023, https://cphn.net/2023/07/05/resignation-letter/; Jack Grove, "Journal Resignations 'Can Drive Scholar-Led Publishing Revolution,'" *Times Higher Education*, June 8, 2023, https://www.timeshighereducation.com/news/journal-resignations-can-drive-scholar-led-publishing-revolution

15. Green and McLaren, "Resignation Letter."

16. Julia Greenberg, "Editors of the Journal Lingua Protest-Quit in Battle for Open Access," *Wired*, 2015, https://www.wired.com/2015/11/editors-of-the-journal-lingua-protest-quit-in-battle-for-open-access/

17. "Zombie Lingua, Elsevier and What Profit-Oriented Publishers Are Good for | Free Science Blog," accessed December 31, 2023, https://www.frank-m-richter.de/freescienceblog/2020/10/03/zombie-lingua-elsevier-and-what-profit-oriented-publishers-are-good-for/

18. Anna Fazackerley, "'Too Greedy': Mass Walkout at Global Science Journal over 'Unethical' Fees," *The Observer*, May 7, 2023, sec. Science, https://www.theguardian.com/science/2023/may/07/too-greedy-mass-walkout-at-global-science-journal-over-unethical-fees

19. Michael Dawson, "#ChiefEditor #Resign @jbiogeography," *Biogeography.News* (blog), June 21, 2023, https://journalofbiogeographynews.org/2023/06/21/chiefeditor-resign-jbiogeography/

20. Sicco de Knecht, "The Death of the Learned Societies?" *ScienceGuide* (blog), June 12, 2019, https://www.scienceguide.nl/2019/06/the-death-of-the-learned-societies/

21. Sara Bosshart, Rod Cookson, and Philipp Hess, "Open Access through Subscribe to Open: A Society Publisher's Implementation," Insights: The UKSG Journal 35, no. 0 (March 16, 2022): 6, https://doi.org/10.1629/uksg.567; Jeffrey Brainard, "New Deals Could Help Scientific Societies Survive Open Access," *Science*, 2019, https://www.science.org/content/article/new-deals-could-help-scientific-societies-survive-open-access

22. https://neuromatch.io/

23. CoARA, "The Agreement Full Text," *CoARA* (blog), 2023, https://coara.eu/agreement/the-agreement-full-text/

24. Rochelle Fritch et al., "Using Narrative CVs: Process Optimization

and Bias Mitigation" (Zenodo, December 22, 2021), https://doi.org/10.5281/ZENODO.5799413

25. Fritch et al., "Using Narrative CVs," 2.

26. Marta Teperek, Maria Cruz, and Danny Kingsley, "Time to Re-Think the Divide between Academic and Support Staff," *Nature*, April 14, 2022, https://doi.org/10.1038/d41586-022-01081-8

27. Nicky Agate et al., "The Transformative Power of Values-Enacted Scholarship," *Humanities and Social Sciences Communications* 7, no. 1 (December 7, 2020): 1–12, https://doi.org/10.1057/s41599-020-00647-z

28. HuMetricsHSS, "Values Framework," accessed July 25, 2024, https://humetricshss.org/our-work/values/

29. Maria Burke, "Pension Deal Agreed for UK Academics but Divisions over Pay Remain Unsolved," *Chemistry World*, October 2023, https://www.chemistryworld.com/news/pension-deal-agreed-for-uk-academics-but-divisions-over-pay-remain-unsolved/4018216.article; Amrei Bahr et al., "With #IchBinHanna, German Academia Protests against a Law That Forces Researchers Out," *Nature Human Behaviour* 5, no. 9 (September 2021): 1114–15, https://doi.org/10.1038/s41562-021-01178-6; "After Historic Strike, UC Grad Students Say University Isn't Honoring Pay Agreements," accessed January 8, 2024, https://www.science.org/content/article/after-historic-strike-uc-grad-students-say-university-isn-t-honoring-pay-agreements

30. Gary Hall, *Digitize This Book! The Politics of New Media, or Why We Need Open Access Now* (Minneapolis: University of Minnesota Press, 2008), 210.

31. Anna McKie, "'Location-Specific' Blocks on Journal Access Could Be OA 'Interim Solution,'" *Times Higher Education*, November 8, 2019, https://www.timeshighereducation.com/news/location-specific-blocks-journal-access-could-be-oa-interim-solution

32. Foo Yun Chee et al., "Europe Agrees Landmark AI Regulation Deal," *Reuters*, December 11, 2023, sec. Technology, https://www.reuters.com/technology/stalled-eu-ai-act-talks-set-resume-2023-12-08/; Karl Vick, "Europe Is Saving Democracy from Big Tech," *TIME*, May 11, 2022, https://time.com/6174614/shoshana-zuboff-twitter-surveillance-capitalism/

33. Rachel Magee, "EU Ready to Back Immediate Open Access without Author Fees," *Research Professional News* (blog), May 5, 2023, https://www.researchprofessionalnews.com/rr-news-europe-infrastructure-2023-5-eu-ready-to-back-immediate-open-access-without-author-fees/

34. Jeff Pooley, "Large Language Publishing," *Upstream* (blog), January 2, 2024, https://doi.org/10.54900/zg929-e9595

Index

"Lili Taylor has always been such a wonderful actor to watch—perhaps partly because of the watchful quality she so often brings to her characters. . . . In *Turning to Birds,* Taylor brings that sharp eye to her own backyard, chronicling her own pleasure at observing the birds at play there. Her enchantment by the various feathered beings whose lives she witnesses may be catching."

—*The Boston Globe*

"A profoundly relatable story about falling in love with the avian world."

—*Audubon*

"Lili Taylor is an actor I've long been in awe of, and now I know why her work has always been soulful and painfully honest. *Turning to Birds* is a treasure map to Taylor's inner life and scripture on how to be truly mindful."

—Griffin Dunne, actor; director; and author of *The Friday Afternoon Club*

"What can an actor—even a consummate one like Lili Taylor—tell us about birding? Plenty, as she brings her profession's keen observation skills to *Turning to Birds,* exploring what our feathered marvels can mean to us people. You couldn't ask for a more personal, accessible approach to the pastime we all love (or will, by the end of this book)."

—Christian Cooper, author of *Better Living Through Birding*

"If you are wondering what this hobby called 'birding' is, why so many people are attracted to it, or how one becomes a birder, wonder no more! In *Turning to Birds,* Lili Taylor answers these questions with flair, insight, and wisdom."

—Douglas W. Tallamy, author of *Nature's Best Hope*

"In a series of lively essays, Taylor dives into her experiences with birds and birding . . . [and] takes the reader along on her journey of discovery. . . . [She] is a wonderful ambassador for our feathered kin."

—*Booklist* (starred review)

"Infectiously exuberant . . . A delightful celebration of the joys of birding—and how it leads one to look at the world in a new light."

—Kirkus Reviews